822.33
T3g

120140

DATE DUE			

Living Shakespeare

THE TRAGEDY OF
KING LEAR

by

William Shakespeare

edited under the supervision of

CARL A. RUDISILL LIBRARY
LENOIR RHYNE COLLEGE

BERNARD GREBANIER

With The New Temple Notes and Glossary

LIVING SHAKESPEARE, INC. • 419 PARK AVE. S. • NEW YORK, N. Y. 10016

INTRODUCTION

King Lear is generally the favorite among Shakespeare's tragedies with those who insist upon singling out one of them as "the greatest." It is not hard to see why. For it touches some of the most basic of human problems: the relation of parents and children, and the terrible pathos of old age. The canvas is vast, and the sufferings, cruelties, and sacrifices of its men and women sweep across it in a mighty tempest. Shelley, with his usual moderation, described it as the most perfect of all human productions.

Nowhere in literature is the conflict between good and evil more fundamental to the work. The play derives much of its power from the violent contrasts it presents between hate and love, cruelty and kindness, devilish wickedness and almost divine goodness. Human nature is revealed at its worst as well as at its best. There are no more terrible fiends in drama than Goneril and Regan; they are an exception among Shakespeare's villains because their wickedness is without motive: they are evil because they love evil. (Such people are, luckily, rare among human beings. But that they do exist the history of the last four decades amply demonstrates.) When we meet the Gonerils and Regans of the world we are, as in *King Lear,* at a loss to account for their stony hearts. Edmund, too, is a wicked fellow—all the more dangerous because he is clever and attractive; but he has at least the faint excuse that he must make his way in the world, though that in no way can justify his villainy.

But if we find in *King Lear* such blood-chilling creatures as Goneril, Regan, Cornwall, Edmund, and Oswald, we also find men and women capable of such goodness as is a tribute to the human race. Some, like Kent, Edgar, and Cordelia, are untiring in their devotion and loyalty to those they love, and in return for injustice have only forgiveness and more love. Some, like Gloucester and Albany, learn from experience that they dare not stand neutral in the war between justice and injustice, and are prepared to sacrifice everything rather than allow wrong to triumph. If *King Lear* shows the wickedness abroad in the world, it also shows the heroic goodness of which humanity is capable.

For those who can listen to the Living Shakespeare recording of *King Lear,* there is one suggestion: because of the limitations of time, the editors of this recording were forced to omit something, and chose to cut much of the Gloucester-Edgar-Edmund subplot. It is important, therefore, if the listener is to do justice to the polyphonic richness of this play, to read the entire text, which is provided herewith. But, as always with Shakespeare, there are peculiar advantages in being able to concentrate upon *hearing* him.

Lear's role is perhaps the most difficult male role in all of drama, and Sir Donald Wolfit's voice is remarkable in its power to communicate all the shades of his temperament, of his decline, of his insanity, of his recovery, and of his last anguished moments. From the outset Sir Donald manages to suggest an old man physically still vigorous and energetic; yet somehow he manages too to make us understand that Lear is at the very twilight of his powers. He is astonishing in the way he has graded Lear's gradual collapse until the moment when, during the fierce storm, he loses his reason. He is uniformly brilliant in portraying the violence of Lear's temper, his pathetic attempts to calm himself and to salvage some dignity. Miss Coral Browne's Goneril is fine in providing, from the outset, the sense of a woman whose interior is in a constant state of rage and tempest. Miss Barbara Jefford's Regan is equally splendid in projecting a woman who is all calm, icy malice. This distinction between the sisters is too often overlooked. Mr. Joseph O'Conor's Gloucester is excellent, and rises to great eloquence in the scene with the Old Man. There are, indeed, numerous passages in this recording which one is not likely ever to forget for their perfection.

BERNARD GREBANIER,
author of *The Heart of Hamlet,* etc.

822.33
+3g
120140
Jan. 1982

PUBLISHER'S NOTE

The full text of King Lear is based on the earliest reliable printed text. In those instances where passages appear only in the First Folio, they are enclosed in brace brackets { }; those which appear only in Quarto are enclosed in square brackets [ ]. Some changes, now universally accepted, were made to meet staging requirements.

The Living Shakespeare acting version of King Lear demanded a number of changes too. There is an occasional shifting of lines, or, more rarely, a word change. Such variations may be observed by comparison with the full text.

For the convenience of readers who wish to use the Living Shakespeare text in conjunction with the Living Shakespeare recording, the acting version is printed in boldface type for easier reading, beginning on page **9.**

© 1962 by Living Shakespeare, Inc.

Library of Congress Catalog Card Number: R62-1148

Printed in the United States of America

THE TRAGEDY OF
KING LEAR

ACTING VERSION
(May be used by schools and amateur groups without permission.)

CAST OF CHARACTERS

LEAR, *King of Britain.*
KING OF FRANCE.
DUKE OF BURGUNDY.
DUKE OF CORNWALL.
DUKE OF ALBANY.
EARL OF KENT.
EARL OF GLOUCESTER.
EDGAR, *Son to* GLOUCESTER.
EDMUND, *Bastard Son to* GLOUCESTER.
CURAN, *a Courtier.*
Old Man, *Tenant to* GLOUCESTER.
Physician.
Fool.
OSWALD, *Steward to* GONERIL.

An Officer *employed by* EDMUND.
Gentleman *attendant on* CORDELIA.
A Herald.
Servants *to* CORNWALL.

GONERIL,
REGAN, } *Daughters to* LEAR.
CORDELIA,

Knights *attending on the* KING, Officers, Messengers, Soldiers, *and* Attendants.

SCENE,—BRITAIN.

ACT ONE

King Lear's palace

Nar. Lear, King of Britain, is old. He decides to divide his kingdom between his three daughters: Goneril, wife of the Duke of Albany; Regan, wife of the Duke of Cornwall; and the youngest, Cordelia, whose suitors are the King of France and the Duke of Burgundy.

Enter Kent, Gloucester, and Edmund

Sennet. Enter one bearing a coronet, King Lear, Cornwall, Albany, Goneril, Regan, Cordelia, and Attendants

Lear. Attend the lords of France and Burgundy, Gloucester.
Glo. I shall, my liege.   *Exeunt Gloucester and Edmund*
Lear. Meantime we shall express our darker purposes;
  Give me the map there. Know that we have divided
  In three our kingdom; and 'tis our fast intent
  To shake all cares and troubles from our age,
  Conferring them on younger strengths, {while we
  Unburthen'd crawl toward death. Our son of Cornwall,
  And you, our no less loving son of Albany,
  We have this hour a constant will to publish
  Our daughters' several dowers, that future strife
  May be prevented now. The princes, France and Burgundy,}

Great rivals in our youngest daughter's love,
Long in our court have made their amorous sojourn,
And here are to be answer'd. Tell me, my daughters,
Which of you shall we say doth love us most,
That we our largest bounty may extend
Where nature doth with merit challenge? Goneril,
  Our eldest-born, speak first.

Gon. Sir, I love you more than words can wield the matter,
  Dearer than eye-sight, space, and liberty,
  Beyond what can be valued, rich or rare,
  No less than life; with grace, health, beauty, honour,
  As much as child e'er loved or father found,
  A love that makes breath poor and speech unable,
  Beyond all manner of so much I love you.

Lear. Of all these bounds, even from this line to this,
  With shadowy forests {and with champains rich'd,
  With plenteous rivers} and wide-skirted meads,
  We make thee lady; to thine and Albany's issues
  Be this perpetual. What says our second daughter?
  Our dearest Regan, wife to Cornwall, speak.

Reg. Sir,
  I am made of that self metal as my sister,
  And prize me at her worth; in my true heart
  I find she names my very deed of love,
  Only she comes too short; that I profess

3

Myself an enemy to all other joys
Which the most precious square of sense possesses,
And find I am alone felicitate
In your dear highness' love.

Lear. To thee and thine hereditary ever
Remain this ample third of our fair kingdom,
No less in space, validity, and pleasure,
Than that conferr'd on Goneril. But now, our joy,
Although the last, not least, {to whose young love,
The vines of France and milk of Burgundy
Strive to be interess'd}, what can you say to draw
A third more opulent than your sisters? {Speak.}

Cord. Nothing, my lord.

{Lear. Nothing?

Cord. Nothing.}

Lear.   Nothing will come of nothing: speak again.

Cord. Unhappy that I am, I cannot heave
My heart into my mouth: I love your majesty
According to my bond, no more nor less.

Lear.   {How, how, Cordelia?} mend your
        speech a little,
Lest it may mar your fortunes.

Cord.   Good my lord,
You have begot me, bred me, lov'd me: I
Return those duties back as are right fit,
Obey you, love you, and most honour you.
Why have my sisters husbands, if they say
They love you all? Haply, when I shall wed,
That lord whose hand must take my plight shall carry
Half my love with him, half my care and duty:
Sure, I shall never marry like my sisters,
To love my father all.

Lear. But goes thy heart with this?

Cord.   Ay, my good lord.

Lear. So young, and so untender?

Cord. So young, my lord, and true.

Lear.   Let it be so, thy truth then be thy dower,
For, by the sacred radiance of the sun,
The mysteries of Hecate, and the night,
By all the operation of the orbs,
From whom we do exist and cease to be,
Here I disclaim all my paternal care,
Propinquity and property of blood,
And as a stranger to my heart and me
Hold thee from this for ever.

Kent.   Good my liege,—

Lear. Peace, Kent!
Come not between the dragon and his wrath;
I lov'd her most, and thought to set my rest
On her kind nursery. Hence, and avoid my sight!
So be my grave my peace, as here I give
Her father's heart from her! Call France; who stirs?
Call Burgundy. Cornwall and Albany,
With my two daughters' dowers digest the third:
Let pride, which she calls plainness, marry her;
I do invest you jointly with my power,
Pre-eminence, and all the large effects
That troop with majesty. Ourself, by monthly course,
With reservation of an hundred knights,
By you to be sustain'd, shall our abode
Make with you by due turn; only we still retain

The name and all the addition to a king;
The sway, revenue, execution of the rest,
Beloved sons, be yours, which to confirm,
This coronet part betwixt you.

Kent.   Royal Lear,
Whom I have ever honour'd·as my king,
Lov'd as my father, as my master follow'd,
As my great patron thought on in my prayers,—

                Reserve thy state,
And in thy best consideration check
This hideous rashness: answer my life my judgement,
Thy youngest daughter does not love thee least;
Nor are those empty-hearted whose low sounds
Reverb no hollowness.

Lear.   Kent, on thy life, no more.

Kent. My life I never held but as a pawn
To wage against thine enemies, nor fear to lose it,
Thy safety being the motive.

Lear.   Hear me, {recreant}
On thy allegiance, hear me!
Since thou hast sought to make us break our vows,
Which we durst never yet, and with strain'd pride
To come between our sentence and our power,
Which nor our nature nor our place can bear,
Our potency made good, take thy reward;
Five days we do allot thee, for provision
To shield thee from diseases of the world,
And on the sixth to turn thy hated back
Upon our kingdom: if on the tenth day following
Thy banish'd trunk be found in our dominions,
The moment is thy death. Away! By Jupiter,
This shall not be revok'd.

Kent. Fare thee well, king, since thus thou wilt appear,
Freedom lives hence, and banishment is here.
(to Cordelia) The gods to their dear shelter take thee,
        maid,
That justly think'st and hast most rightly said!
(to Regan and Goneril) And your large speeches may
        your deeds approve,
That good effects may spring from words of love.
Thus Kent, O princes, bids you all adieu;
He 'll shape his old course in a country new.   Exit

*Flourish. Re-enter Gloucester, with France, Burgundy,
        and Attendants*

Glo. Here 's France and Burgundy, my noble lord.

Lear. My lord of Burgundy,
We first address toward you, who with this king
Hath rivall'd for our daughter, what, in the least,
Will you require in present dower with her,
Or cease your quest of love?

Bur.   Most royal majesty,
I crave no more than hath your highness offer'd,
Nor will you tender less.

Lear.   Right noble Burgundy,
When she was dear to us, we did hold her so;
But now her price is fall'n. Sir, there she stands:
If aught within that little seeming substance,
Or all of it, with our displeasure piec'd,
And nothing more, may fitly like your grace,
She 's there, and she is yours.

Bur.   Pardon me, royal sir,
  Election makes not up on such conditions.
Lear. Then leave her, sir, for, by the power that made me,
  I tell you all her wealth. (to France) For you, great
    king,
  I would not from your love make such a stray,
  To match you where I hate; therefore beseech you
  To avert your liking a more worthier way
  Than on a wretch whom nature is asham'd
  Almost to acknowledge hers.
Fra. Fairest Cordelia, that art most rich being poor,
  Most choice forsaken, and most lov'd despis'd,
  Thy dowerless daughter, king, thrown to my chance,
  Is queen of us, of ours, and our fair France:
  Not all the dukes of waterish Burgundy
  Shall buy this unpriz'd precious maid of me.
  Bid them farewell, Cordelia, though unkind:
  Thou losest here, a better where to find.
Lear. Thou hast her, France, let her be thine, for we
  Have no such daughter, nor shall ever see
  That face of hers again. Therefore be gone,
  Without our grace, our love, our benison.
  Come, noble Burgundy.
                                        Flourish. Exeunt.

Nar. Cordelia leaves Britain to become Queen of France.
  Lear goes first with his hundred knights to stay with
  Goneril and her husband, Albany.

                    The Duke of Albany's palace

              Enter Goneril and Oswald, her steward

Gon. By day and night he wrongs me; every hour
  He flashes into one gross crime or other,
  That sets us all at odds: I'll not endure it:
  His knights grow riotous, and himself upbraids us
  On every trifle. When he returns from hunting,
  I will not speak with him; say I am sick:
  If you come slack of former services,
  You shall do well; the fault of it I'll answer.
Osw. He's coming, madam, I hear him.   *Horns within*
Gon. Put on what weary negligence you please,
  You and your fellows; I'ld have it come to question:
  If he distaste it, let him to my sister,
  Whose mind and mine, I know, in that are one,
Gon. And let his knights have colder looks among you;
  What grows of it, no matter; advise your fellows so.

                    A hall in the same

      Horns within. Enter Lear, Knights, and Attendants,
                  Fool,   Goneril.

Lear. How now, daughter, what makes that frontlet on?
  Methinks you are too much of late i' the frown.
Fool. Thou wast a pretty fellow when thou hadst no need
  to care for her frowning; now thou art an O without a
  figure: I am better than thou art now; I am a fool, thou
  art nothing. Yes, forsooth, I will hold my tongue; so
  your face bids me, though you say nothing.

    Mum, mum:
      He that keeps nor crust nor crumb,
      Weary of all, shall want some.
    (*pointing to Lear*) That's a sheal'd peascod.
Gon. Not only, sir, this, your all-licens'd fool,
  But other of your insolent retinue,
  Do hourly carp and quarrel, breaking forth
  In rank and not to be endured riots.
Fool. For, you know, nuncle,
      The hedge-sparrow fed the cuckoo so long,
      That it had it head bit off by it young.
  So out went the candle, and we were left darkling.
Lear. Are you our daughter?
Gon. I would you would make use of your good wisdom
  Whereof I know you are fraught, and put away
  These dispositions which of late transport you
  From what you rightly are.
Fool. May not an ass know when the cart draws the horse?
  Whoop, Jug, I love thee.
Lear. Doth any here know me?   This is not Lear:
  Doth Lear walk thus? speak thus?
  Who is that can tell me who I am?
Fool. Lear's shadow.
Gon. I do beseech you
  To understand my purposes aright;
  As you are old and reverend, should be wise.
  Here do you keep a hundred knights and squires,
  Men so disorder'd, so debosh'd and bold,
  That this our court, infected with their manners,
  Shows like a riotous inn: epicurism and lust
  Make it more like a tavern or brothel
  Than a grac'd palace. The shame itself doth speak
  For instant remedy: be then desir'd
  By her, that else will take the thing she begs,
  A little to disquantity your train,
  And the remainder that shall still depend,
  To be such men as may besort your age,
  Which know themselves and you.
Lear.   Darkness, and devils!
  Saddle my horses, call my train together.
  Degenerate bastard, I'll not trouble thee:
  Yet have I left a daughter.
{Alb.   Pray, sir, be patient.}
Lear. My train are men of choice and rarest parts,
  That all particulars of duty know,
  And in the most exact regard support
  The worships of their name. O most small fault,
  How ugly didst thou in Cordelia show!
  Which, like an engine, wrench'd my frame of nature
  From the fix'd place, drew from my heart all love
  And added to the gall. O Lear, Lear, Lear,
  Beat at this gate, that let thy folly in
                                        Striking his head
  And thy dear judgement out! Go, go, my people,
Alb. My lord, I am guiltless, as I am ignorant
  {Of what hath mov'd you.}
Lear.   It may be so, my lord [of Albany.]
  Hear, Nature, hear, dear goddess, hear!
  Suspend thy purpose, if thou didst intend
  To make this creature fruitful;

Turn all her mother's pains and benefits
To laughter and contempt, that she may feel
How sharper than a serpent's tooth it is
To have a thankless child! Away, away. *Exit*

Enter Oswald

How now, Oswald?

What, have you writ that letter to my sister?
Osw. Ay, madam.
Gon. Take you some company, and away to horse,
Inform her full of my particular fear,
And thereto add such reasons of your own
As may compact it more. Get you gone;
And hasten your return. (*exit Oswald.*)

ACT TWO

Nar. On receipt of Goneril's letter, Regan and her husband, Cornwall, unwilling to receive the king, hasten to the castle of the Earl of Gloucester, where Lear follows them. They refuse to see him.

Before Gloucester's castle.

Enter Lear, with Gloucester.

Lear. Deny to speak with me? They 're sick? they 're weary?
They have travell'd all the night?
Fetch me a better answer.
Glo.   My dear lord,
You know the fiery quality of the duke;
How unremovable and fix'd he is
In his own course.
Lear. Vengeance, plague, death, confusion!
Fiery? What quality? Why, Gloucester, Gloucester,
I 'ld speak with the Duke of Cornwall, and his wife.
{Glo. Well, my good lord, I have inform'd them so.
Lear. Inform'd them! Dost thou understand me, man?}
Glo. Ay, my good lord.
Lear. The king would speak with Cornwall; the dear father
Would with his daughter speak, commands her service:
{Are they inform'd of this? My breath and blood!}
Go tell the duke and 's wife I 'ld speak with them,
Now, presently; bid them come forth and hear me,
Or at their chamber-door I 'll beat the drum
Till it cry sleep to death.
                    Exit Gloucester

Kent is set at liberty

Reg. I am glad to see your highness.
Lear. Regan, I think you are; I know what reason
I have to think so; if thou shouldst not be glad,
I would divorce me from thy mother's tomb,
Sepulchring an adultress.
                    Beloved Regan,
Thy sister is naught, she hath tied
Sharp-tooth'd unkindness, like a vulture, here:
                    Points to his heart
I can scarce speak to thee, thou 'lt not believe

With how deprav'd a quality—O Regan!
Reg. I pray you, sir, take patience: I have hope
You less know how to value her desert
Than she to scant her duty.
{Lear.   Say, how is that?
Reg. I cannot think my sister in the least
Would fail her obligation: if, sir, perchance
She have restrain'd the riots of your followers,
'Tis on such ground and to such wholesome end
As clears her from all blame.}
Lear. My curses on her!
Reg.   O, sir, you are old;
Nature in you stands on the very verge
Of her confine; you should be rul'd and led
By some discretion that discerns your state
Better than you yourself. Therefore I pray you
That to our sister you do make return;
Say you have wrong'd her, sir.
Lear.   Ask her forgiveness?
Do you mark how this becomes the house:
(*kneeling*) "Dear daughter, I confess that I am old,
Age is unnecessary, on my knees I beg
That you 'll vouchsafe me raiment, bed and food."
Reg. Good sir, no more; these are unsightly tricks:
Return you to my sister.
Lear.   (*rising*) Never, Regan:
She hath abated me of half my train,
Look'd black upon me, struck me with her tongue,
Most serpent-like, upon the very heart:
All the stor'd vengeances of heaven fall
On her ingrateful top! Strike her young bones,
You taking airs, with lameness.
Corn.   Fie, sir, fie!
Lear. You nimble lightnings, dart your blinding flames
Into her scornful eyes, infect her beauty,
You fen-suck'd fogs, drawn by the powerful sun,
To fall and blast her pride.
Reg. O the blest gods! so will you wish on me,
When the rash mood is on.
Lear. No, Regan, thou shalt never have my curse:
Thy tender-hefted nature shall not give
Thee o'er to harshness; her eyes are fierce, but thine
Do comfort and not burn. 'Tis not in thee
To grudge my pleasures, to cut off my train,
To bandy hasty words, to scant my sizes,

And, in conclusion, to oppose the bolt
Against my coming in; thou better know'st
The offices of nature, bond of childhood,
Thy half o' the kingdom hast thou not forgot,
Wherein I thee endow'd.

Tucket within

Corn.   What trumpet 's that?
Reg. I know 't my sister's: this approves her letter,
That she would soon be here.

Enter Oswald, Goneril

Lear.   Who comes here? O heavens,
If you do love old men, if your sweet sway
Allow obedience, if yourselves are old,
Make it your cause; send down, and take my part!
(*to Gon.*) Art not asham'd to look upon this beard?
O Regan, wilt thou take her by the hand?
Gon. Why not by the hand, sir? How have I offended?
All 's not offence that indiscretion finds
And dotage terms so.
Lear.   O sides, you are too tough,
Will you yet hold?
Reg. I pray you, father, being weak, seem so.
If, till the expiration of your month,
You will return and sojourn with my sister,
Dismissing half your train, come then to me:
I am now from home and out of that provision
Which shall be needful for your entertainment.
Lear. Return to her, and fifty men dismiss'd?
Persuade me rather to be slave and sumpter
To this detested groom.   *Pointing at Oswald*
Gon.   At your choice, sir.
Lear.   I prithee, daughter, do not make me mad;
I will not trouble thee, my child; farewell:
We 'll no more meet, no more see one another:
But yet thou art my flesh, my blood, my daughter,
Or rather a disease that 's in my flesh,
Which I must needs call mine;
I can be patient, I can stay with Regan,
I and my hundred knights.
Reg.   Not altogether so:
I look'd not for you yet, nor am provided
For your fit welcome. Give ear, sir, to my sister.
If you will come to me,

For now I spy a danger, I entreat you
To bring but five and twenty, to no more
Will I give place or notice.
Lear. I gave you all—
Reg.   And in good time you gave it.
Lear. Made you my guardians, my depositaries,
But kept a reservation to be follow'd
With such a number. What, must I come to you
With five and twenty; Regan, said you so?
Reg. And speak 't again, my lord, no more with me.
Lear.   (*to Gon.*) [Then Goneril,]
I 'll go with thee,
Thy fifty yet doth double five and twenty,
And thou art twice her love.
Gon.   Hear me, my lord:
What need you five and twenty, ten, or five,
To follow in a house where twice so many
Have a command to tend you?
Reg.   What need one?
Lear. O, reason not the need: our basest beggars
Are in the poorest things superfluous:
Allow not nature more than nature needs,
Man's life is cheap as beast's.
          But for true need,—
You heavens, give me that patience, patience I need!
You see me here, you gods, a poor old man,
As full of grief as age, wretched in both:
If it be you that stir these daughters' hearts
Against their father, fool me not so much
To bear it tamely; touch me with noble anger,
And let not women's weapons, water-drops,
Stain my man's cheeks! No, you unnatural hags,
I will have such revenges on you both
That all the world shall—I will do such things,—
What they are, yet I know not, but they shall be
The terrors of the earth. You think I 'll weep;
No, I 'll not weep: I have full cause of weeping,

Storm and tempest

But this heart shall break into a hundred thousand
    flaws,
Or ere I 'll weep. O fool, I shall go mad!

Exeunt

ACT THREE

Nar. The King, with only his fool for company, leaves the castle and wanders out into the stormy night.

A heath

Storm still. Enter Lear and Fool

Lear. Blow, winds, and crack your cheeks! rage! blow!
You cataracts and hurricanoes, spout
Till you have drench'd our steeples, drown'd the cocks!
You sulphurous and thought-executing fires,

Vaunt-couriers of oak-cleaving thunderbolts,
Singe my white head! And thou, all-shaking thunder,
Smite flat the thick rotundity o' the world,
Crack nature's moulds, all germins spill at once
That make ingrateful man!

Fool. O nuncle, court holy-water in a dry house is better than this rain-water out o' door. Good nuncle, in; ask thy daughters' blessing; here 's a night pities neither wise men nor fools.

Lear. Rumble thy bellyful! Spit, fire! spout, rain!
    Nor rain, wind, thunder, fire, are my daughters:
    I tax not you, you elements, with unkindness,
    I never gave you kingdom, call'd you children,
    You owe me no subscription: then, let fall
    Your horrible pleasure; here I stand, your slave,
    A poor, infirm, weak and despis'd old man;
    But yet I call you servile ministers,
    That have with two pernicious daughters join'd
    Your high-engender'd battles 'gainst a head
    So old and white as this. O! 'tis foul!

Fool. He that has a house to put his head in has a good
    head-piece.

Nar. Although banished, the faithful Kent, disguised as a
    servant, has followed the King.

Enter Kent

Kent. Alas, sir, are you here? things that love night
    Love not such nights as these; the wrathful skies
    Gallow the very wanderers of the dark,
    And make them keep their caves: since I was man,
    Such sheets of fire, such bursts of horrid thunder,
    Such groans of roaring wind and rain, I never
    Remember to have heard: man's nature cannot carry
    The affliction nor the fear.

Lear.   Let the great gods,
    That keep this dreadful pother o'er our heads,
    Find out their enemies now. Tremble, thou wretch,
    That hast within thee undivulged crimes,
    Unwhipp'd of justice: hide thee, thou bloody hand,
    Thou perjur'd, and thou simular man of virtue
    That art incestuous.

                            I am a man
    More sinn'd against than sinning.

Kent. Gracious my lord, hard by here is a hovel;
    Some friendship will it lend you 'gainst the tempest:
    Repose you there, whilst I to this hard house—
    More harder than the stones whereof 'tis rais'd;
                        —return, and force
    Their scanted courtesy.

Lear.   My wits begin to turn.
    Come on, my boy: how dost, my boy? art cold?
    I am cold myself; where is this straw, my fellow?
    The art of our necessities is strange,
    That can make vile things precious. Come, your hovel.
    Poor fool and knave, I have one part in my heart
    That 's sorry yet for thee.

Fool. (*singing*)
            He that has a little tiny wit,—
            With hey, ho, the wind and the rain,—
            Must make content with his fortunes fit,
            Though the rain it raineth every day.

Lear. True, my good boy. Come, bring us to this hovel.
                                                    Exeunt

The heath. Before a hovel
Enter Lear, Kent, and Fool

Kent. Here is the place, my lord, good my lord, enter.

Storm still

Lear. Prithee, go in thyself, seek thine own ease:
    This tempest will not give me leave to ponder
    On things would hurt me more. But I 'll go in.
    {(*to the Fool*) In boy; go first. You houseless poverty,—
    Nay, get thee in. I 'll pray, and then I 'll sleep.}
                                                Fool goes in
    Poor naked wretches, wheresoe'er you are,
    That bide the pelting of this pitiless storm,
    How shall your houseless heads, and unfed sides,
    Your loop'd and window'd raggedness, defend you
    From seasons such as these? O, I have ta'en
    Too little care of this! Take physic, pomp,
    Expose thyself to feel what wretches feel,
    That thou mayst shake the superflux to them
    And show the heavens more just.

Nar. The fool goes into the hovel, but rushes out again,
    terrified. He has found a seeming madman, poor Tom
    —in reality Edgar, son of the Earl of Gloucester, in dis-
    guise. For Gloucester's bastard son, Edmund, has per-
    suaded his father that Edgar is plotting to kill him.
                        The Fool runs out from the hovel}

Fool. Come not in here, nuncle, here 's a spirit.
    Help me, help me!

Kent. Give me thy hand, who 's there?

Fool. A spirit, a spirit; he says his name 's poor Tom.

Kent. What art thou that dost grumble there i' the straw?
    Come forth.

Enter Edgar disguised as a madman

Edg. Away! the foul fiend follows me!
    "Through the sharp hawthorn blow the winds."
    Go to thy bed and warm thee.

Lear. Hast thou given all to thy two daughters, and art
    thou come to this?

Storm still

Fool. Nay, he reserv'd a blanket, else we had been all
    sham'd.

Lear. Now, all the plagues that in the pendulous air
    Hang fated o'er men's faults light on thy daughters!

Kent. He hath no daughters, sir.

Lear. Death, traitor! nothing could have subdued nature
    To such a lowness but his unkind daughters;
    Is it the fashion that discarded fathers
    Should have thus little mercy on their flesh?
    Judicious punishment! 'twas this flesh begot
    Those pelican daughters.

Edg.   Pilicock sat on Pelicock-hill:
                Alow, alow, loo, loo!

Fool. This cold night will turn us all to fools and mad-
    men.
                                                    Exeunt

ACT FOUR

Nar. Gloucester finds them at the hovel and urges Kent to take the King at once to Dover, where Cordelia has landed with a French army. The bastard, Edmund, denounces his father to Regan as a traitor, and on her orders, Gloucester is seized and his eyes are burnt out. He wanders blindly through the countryside, led by an Old Man.

The heath

*Enter Edgar and
Gloucester, led by an Old Man.*

O.M. O, my good lord, I have been your tenant, and your father's tenant, this four-score years.

Glo. Away, get thee away; good friend, be gone:
Thy comforts can do me no good at all,
Thee they may hurt.

O.M.   You cannot see your way.

Glo. I have no way, and therefore want no eyes;
I stumbled when I saw; full oft 'tis seen,
Our means secure us, and our mere defects
Prove our commodities. Ah, dear son Edgar,
The food of thy abused father's wrath!
Might I but live to see thee in my touch,
I 'ld say I had eyes again!

Edg.   But who comes here?
My father, poorly led? World, world, O world!
But that thy strange mutations make us hate thee,
Life would not yield to age.

O.M.   How now, who 's there?

Edg. [Poor Tom's a-cold.]

O.M.   'Tis poor mad Tom.

O.M. Fellow, where goest?

Glo.   Is it a beggar-man?

O.M. Madman, and beggar too.

Glo. He has some reason, else he could not beg.
I' the last night's storm I such a fellow saw,
Which made me think a man a worm; my son
Came then into my mind, and yet my mind
Was then scarce friends with him: I have heard more
  since.
As flies to wanton boys, are we to the gods;
They kill us for their sport.   *Exit Old Man*

Glo. Come hither, fellow.

Edg.   —Bless thy sweet eyes, they
  bleed.

Glo. Know'st thou the way to Dover?

Edg. Ay, master.

Glo. There is a cliff whose high and bending head
Looks fearfully in the confined deep:
Bring me but to the very brim of it,
And I 'll repair the misery thou dost bear
With something rich about me; from that place
I shall no leading need.

Edg.   Give me thy arm:
Poor Tom shall lead thee.   *Exeunt*

The French camp near Dover

Nar. At Dover, Cordelia has heard news of her father.

A tent

*Enter, with drum and colours, Cordelia, Doctor,
and Soldiers*

Cord. Alack, 'tis he: why, he was met even now
As mad as the vex'd sea, singing aloud,
Crown'd with rank fumiter and furrow-weeds.
                    A century send forth;
Search every acre in the high-grown field,
And bring him to our eye. [*exit an Officer*] What can
  man's wisdom
In the restoring his bereaved sense?
He that helps him take all my outward worth.

Doc. There is means, madame:
Our foster-nurse of nature is repose,
The which he lacks; that to provoke in him,
Are many simples operative, whose power
Will close the eye of anguish.

Cord.   All blest secrets,
All you unpublish'd virtues of the earth,
Spring with my tears!
                    Seek, seek for him,
Lest his ungovern'd rage dissolve the life
That wants the means to lead it.

Enter a Messenger

Mes.   News, madam;
The British powers are marching hitherward.

Cord. 'Tis known before; our preparation stands
In expectation of them. O dear father,
It is thy business that I go about;
Soon may I hear and see him!   *Exeunt*

Nar. King Lear is found and placed in the care of a doctor.

*A tent in the French camp. Lear on a bed asleep, soft
music playing; Gentleman, and others standing*

Enter Cordelia, Kent, and Doctor

Cord.   (*to the Doctor*) How does
  the king?

Doc. Madame, sleeps still.

Cord. O my dear father! Restoration hang
Thy medicine on my lips, and let this kiss
Repair those violent harms that my two sisters
Have in thy reverence made!
Had you not been their father, these white flakes
Had challenged pity of them. Was this a face
To be expos'd against the warring winds?
                    He wakes; speak to him.

Doc. Madam, do you; 'tis fittest.

Cord. How does my royal lord? How fares your majesty?
Lear. You do me wrong to take me out o' the grave:
  Thou art a soul in bliss, but I am bound
  Upon a wheel of fire, that mine own tears
  Do scald like molten lead.
Cord.   Sir, do you know me?
Lear. You are a spirit, I know, where did you die?
Cord. Still, still, far wide!
Doc. He 's scarce awake, let him alone awhile.
Lear. Where have I been? Where am I? Fair daylight?
  I am mightily abus'd. I should e'en die with pity,
  To see another thus. I know not what to say.
  I will not swear these are my hands: let 's see;
  I feel this pin prick. Would I were assur'd
  Of my condition!
Cord.   O, look upon me, sir,
  And hold your hands in benediction o'er me.
  No, sir, you must not kneel.
Lear.   Pray, do not mock me.
  I am a very foolish fond old man,
  Fourscore and upward, {not an hour more nor less;}
  And, to deal plainly,

I fear I am not in my perfect mind.
Methinks I should know you, and know this man;
Yet I am doubtful, for I am mainly ignorant
What place this is, and all the skill I have
Remembers not these garments, nor I know not
Where I did lodge last night. Do not laugh at me,
For, as I am a man, I think this lady
To be my child Cordelia.
Cord.   And so I am, I am.
Lear. Be your tears wet? yes, faith. I pray, weep not:
  If you have poison for me, I will drink it.
  I know you do not love me, for your sisters
  Have, as I do remember, done me wrong:
  You have some cause, they have not.
Cord.   No cause, no cause.
Lear. Am I in France?
Kent.   In your own kingdom, sir.
Lear. Do not abuse me.
Cord. Will 't please your highness walk?
Lear.   You must bear with me.
  Pray now, forget and forgive: I am old and foolish.
                     Exeunt

ACT FIVE

The British camp near Dover

Nar. The British forces, under the command of Edmund, defeat the French. King Lear and Cordelia are taken prisoner.

A field between the two camps

Enter, in conquest, with drum and colours, Edmund; Lear and Cordelia, as prisoners; Captain, Soldiers, etc.

Edm. Some officers take them away.
Cord.   We are not the first
  Who with best meaning have incurr'd the worst.
  For thee, oppressed king, am I cast down;
  Myself could else out-frown false fortune's frown.
  Shall we not see these daughters, and these sisters?
Lear. No, no, no, no! Come, let 's away to prison:
  We two alone will sing like birds i' the cage:
  When thou dost ask me blessing, I 'll kneel down
  And ask of thee forgiveness: so we 'll live,
  And pray, and sing, and tell old tales, and laugh
  At gilded butterflies, and hear poor rogues
  Talk of court news; and we 'll talk with them too,
  Who loses and who wins, who 's in, who 's out,
  And take upon 's the mystery of things,
  As if we were God's spies; and we 'll wear out,
  In a wall'd prison, packs and sects of great ones
  That ebb and flow by the moon.
Edm.   Take them away.

Lear. He that parts us shall bring a brand from heaven,
  And fire us hence like foxes. Wipe thine eyes;
  The good years shall devour them, flesh and fell,
  Ere they shall make us weep: we 'll see 'em starve first.
  Come.   *Exeunt Lear and Cordelia, guarded*

Nar. The Duke of Cornwall is dead, and Edmund holds power in Britain. Both Regan and Goneril want to marry Edmund, and in her jealousy Goneril poisons Regan and stabs herself. Cordelia is hanged on Edmund's orders, and Lear bears her in his arms.

Enter Lear, with Cordelia in his arms; Edgar, Captain, and others following

Lear. Howl, howl, howl, howl! O, you are men of stones:
  Had I your tongues and eyes, I 'ld use them so
  That heaven's vault should crack. She 's gone for ever!
  I know when one is dead and when one lives;
  She 's dead as earth. Lend me a looking-glass,
  If that her breath will mist or stain the stone,
  Why then she lives.
Kent.   Is this the promis'd end?
Edg. Or image of that horror?
Alb.   Fall and cease.
Lear. This feather stirs, she lives; if it be so,
  It is a chance which does redeem all sorrows
  That ever I have felt.
Kent.   Ah my good master!
Lear. Prithee, away.
Edg.   'Tis noble Kent, your friend.

[Kent. Peace, good Edgar.]

Lear. A plague upon you murderers, traitors all!
    I might have sav'd her; now she 's gone for ever!
    Cordelia, Cordelia, stay a little. Ha!
    What is 't thou say'st? Her voice was ever soft,
    Gentle and low, an excellent thing in woman.
    I kill'd the slave that was a-hanging thee.

Enter a Captain

Capt. [My lord of Albany,] Edmund is dead.

Alb.   That 's but a trifle here.
    You lords and noble friends, know our intent.
    What comfort to this great decay may come
    Shall be applied: for us, we will resign,
    During the life of this old majesty,
    To him our absolute power.
    (to Edgar and Kent) All friends shall taste
    The wages of their virtue, and all foes
    The cup of their deservings. O, see, see!

Lear. And my poor fool is hang'd! No, no, no life!
    Why should a dog, a horse, a rat, have life,
    And thou no breath at all? Thou 'lt come no more;
    Never, never, never. {never, never.}

Pray you, undo this button: thank you, sir.
          {Do you see this! Look on her, look,
  her lips,
    Look there, look there!}   *Lear dies*

Edg.   He faints. My lord, my lord!

Kent. Break, heart; I prithee, break!

Edg.   Look up, my lord.

Kent. Vex not his ghost: O, let him pass! he hates him
    That would upon the rack of this tough world
    Stretch him out longer.

Edg.   He is gone indeed.

Kent. The wonder is he hath endur'd so long:
    He but usurp'd his life.

Alb.   *(to Kent and Edgar)* Friends of my soul,
    you twain
    Rule in this realm and the gor'd state sustain.

Kent. I have a journey, sir, shortly to go;
    My master calls me; I must not say no.

Edg. The weight of this sad time we must obey,
    Speak what we feel, not what we ought to say.

Alb. The oldest have borne most: we that are young
    Shall never see so much, nor live so long.

Exeunt, with a dead march

FULL TEXT

Act First

SCENE I

King Lear's palace

Enter Kent, Gloucester, and Edmund

Kent. I thought the King had more affected the Duke of Albany than Cornwall.

Glo. It did always seem so to us, but now, in the division of the kingdoms, it appears not which of the dukes he values most, for equalities are so weighed, that curiosity in neither can make choice of either's moiety.

Kent. Is not this your son, my lord?

Glo. His breeding, sir, hath been at my charge; I have so often blush'd to acknowledge him, that now I am braz'd to it. 10

Kent. I cannot conceive you.

Glo. Sir, this young fellow's mother could, whereupon she grew round-wombed, and had indeed, sir, a son for her cradle ere she had a husband for her bed. Do you smell a fault?

Kent. I cannot wish the fault undone, the issue of it being so proper.

Glo. But I have, sir, a son by order of law, some year elder than this, who yet is no dearer in my account: 20 though this knave came something saucily into the world before he was sent for, yet was his mother fair, there was good sport at his making, and the whoreson must be acknowledged. Do you know this noble gentleman, Edmund?

Edm. No, my lord.

Glo. My lord of Kent: remember him hereafter as my honourable friend.

Edm. My services to your lordship.

Kent. I must love you, and sue to know you better. 30

Edm. Sir, I shall study deserving.

Glo. He hath been out nine years, and away he shall again. The King is coming.

Sennet. Enter one bearing a coronet, King Lear, Cornwall, Albany, Goneril, Regan, Cordelia, and Attendants

Lear. Attend my lords of France and Burgundy, Gloucester.

Glo. I shall, my liege. *Exeunt Gloucester and Edmund*

Lear. Meantime we will express our darker purposes;
The map there. Know we have divided
In three our kingdom; and 'tis our first intent
To shake all cares and business off our state,
Confirming them on younger years, {while we 40
Unburthen'd crawl toward death. Our son of Cornwall,
And you, our no less loving son of Albany,
We have this hour a constant will to publish
Our daughters' several dowers, that future strife
May be prevented now. The princes, France and Burgundy,}
The two great princes, France and Burgundy,
Great rivals in our youngest daughter's love,
Long in our court have made their amorous sojourn,
And here are to be answer'd. Tell me, my daughters,
{Since now we will divest us both of rule, 50
Interest of territory, cares of state,}
Which of you shall we say doth love us most,
That we our largest bounty may extend
Where merit doth most challenge it? Goneril,
Our eldest-born, speak first.

Gon. Sir, I do love you more than words can wield the matter,
Dearer than eye-sight, space, or liberty,
Beyond what can be valued, rich or rare,
No less than life; with grace, health, beauty, honour,

As much as child e'er loved or father found, 60
A love that makes breath poor and speech unable,
Beyond all manner of so much I love you.

Cord. (aside) What shall Cordelia do? Love, and be silent.

Lear. Of all these bounds, even from this line to this,
With shady forests {and with champains rich'd,
With plenteous rivers} and wide-skirted meads,
We make thee lady; to thine and Albany's issue
Be this perpetual. What says our second daughter?
Our dearest Regan, wife to Cornwall, speak.

Reg. Sir, I am made 70
Of the self-same metal that my sister is,
And prize me at her worth; in my true heart
I find she names my very deed of love,
Only she came short; that I profess
Myself an enemy to all other joys
Which the most precious square of sense possesses,
And find I am alone felicitate
In your dear highness' love.

Cord. (aside) Then poor Cordelia!
And yet not so, since I am sure my love's
More richer than my tongue. 80

Lear. To thee and thine hereditary ever
Remain this ample third of our fair kingdom,
No less in space, validity, and pleasure,
Than that confirm'd on Goneril. But now, our joy,
Although the last, not least in our dear love.
What can you say to win
A third more opulent than your sisters?

Cord. Nothing, my lord.

{*Lear.* Nothing!

Cord. Nothing.}

Lear. How? Nothing will come of nothing: speak again. 90

Cord. Unhappy that I am, I cannot heave
My heart into my mouth: I love your majesty
According to my bond, nor more nor less.

Lear. Go to, go to, mend your speech a little,
Lest it may mar your fortunes.

Cord. Good my lord,
You have begot me, bred me, lov'd me: I
Return those duties back as are right fit,
Obey you, love you, and most honour you.
Why have my sisters husbands, if they say 100
They love you all? Haply, when I shall wed,
That lord whose hand must take my plight shall carry
Half my love with him, half my care and duty:
Sure, I shall never marry like my sisters,
To love my father all.

Lear. But goes this with thy heart?

Cord. Ay, good my lord.

Lear. So young, and so untender?

Cord. So young, my lord, and true.

Lear. Well, let it be so, thy truth then be thy dower,
For, by the sacred radiance of the sun, 110
The mysteries of Hecat, and the night,
By all the operation of the orbs,
From whom we do exist and cease to be,
Here I disclaim all my paternal care,
Propinquity and property of blood,
And as a stranger to my heart and me
Hold thee from this for ever. The barbarous Scythian,
Or he that makes his generation
Messes to gorge his appetite, shall be
As well neighbour'd, pitied and reliev'd, 120
As thou my sometime daughter.

Kent. Good my liege,—

Lear. Peace, Kent!
Come not between the dragon and his wrath;
I lov'd her most, and thought to set my rest
On her kind nursery. Hence, and avoid my sight!

So be my grave my peace, as here I give
Her father's heart from her! Call France; who stirs?
Call Burgundy. Cornwall and Albany,
With my two daughters' dowers digest this third:
Let pride, which she calls plainness, marry her; 130
I do invest you jointly in my power,
Pre-eminence, and all the large effects
That troop with majesty. Ourself, by monthly course,
With reservation of an hundred knights,
By you to be sustain'd, shall our abode
Make with you by due turns; only we still retain
The name and all the additions to a king;
The sway, revenue, execution of the rest,
Beloved sons, be yours, which to confirm,
This coronet part betwixt you.

Kent. Royal Lear, 140
Whom I have ever honour'd as my king,
Lov'd as my father, as my master follow'd,
As my great patron thought on in my prayers,—

Lear. The bow is bent and drawn; make from the shaft.

Kent. Let it fall rather, though the fork invade
The region of my heart: be Kent unmannerly,
When Lear is mad. What wilt thou do, old man?
Think'st thou that duty shall have dread to speak,
When power to flattery bows? To plainness honour's bound,
When majesty stoops to folly. Reverse thy doom, 150
And in thy best consideration check
This hideous rashness: answer my life my judgement,
Thy youngest daughter does not love thee least;
Nor are those empty-hearted whose low sound
Reverbs no hollowness.

Lear. Kent, on thy life, no more.

Kent. My life I never held but as a pawn
To wage against thy enemies, nor fear to lose it,
Thy safety being the motive.

Lear. Out of my sight!

Kent. See better, Lear, and let me still remain
The true blank of thine eye. 160

Lear. Now, by Apollo,—

Kent. Now, by Apollo, king,
Thou swear'st thy gods in vain.

Lear. Vassal! recreant!
Laying his hand on his sword

{*Alb.*}
Corn. } Dear sir, forbear.}

Kent. Do;
Kill thy physician, and the fee bestow
Upon the foul disease; revoke thy doom,
Or, whilst I can vent clamour from my throat,
I'll tell thee thou dost evil.

Lear. Hear me,
On thy allegiance, hear me!
Since thou hast sought to make us break our vow, 170
Which we durst never yet, and with stray'd pride
To come between our sentence and our power,
Which nor our nature nor our place can bear,
Our potency made good, take thy reward;
Four days we do allot thee, for provision
To shield thee from diseases of the world,
And on the fifth to turn thy hated back
Upon our kingdom: if on the tenth day following
Thy banish'd trunk be found in our dominions,
The moment is thy death. Away! By Jupiter, 180
This shall not be revok'd.

Kent. Why, fare thee well, king, since thus thou wilt appear,
Friendship lives hence, and banishment is here.
(to Cordelia) The gods to their protection take thee, maid,
That rightly thinks and hast most justly said!

(to Regan *and* Goneril*)* And your large speeches may
    your deeds approve,
That good effects may spring from words of love.
Thus Kent, O princes, bids you all adieu ;
He 'll shape his old course in a country new.   *Exit*
    Flourish. Re-enter Gloucester, with France, Burgundy,
        and Attendants
Glo. Here 's France and Burgundy, my noble lord.   190
Lear. My lord of Burgundy,
    We first address towards you, who with a king
    Hath rivall'd for our daughter, what, in the least,
    Will you require in present dower with her,
    Or cease your quest of love ?
Bur.   Royal majesty,
    I crave no more than what your highness offer'd,
    Nor will you tender less.
Lear.   Right noble Burgundy,
    When she was dear to us, we did hold her so ;
    But now her price is fall'n. Sir, there she stands :
    If aught within that little seeming substance,   200
    Or all of it, with our displeasure piec'd,
    And nothing else, may fitly like your grace,
    She 's there, and she is yours.
Bur.   I know no answer.
Lear. Sir, will you, with those infirmities she owes,
    Unfriended, new adopted to our hate,
    Cover'd with our curse and stranger'd with our oath,
    Take her, or leave her ?
Bur.   Pardon me, royal sir,
    Election makes not up on such conditions.
Lear. Then leave her, sir, for, by the power that made me,
    I tell you all her wealth. *(to* France*)* For you, great
      king,   210
    I would not from your love make such a stray,
    To match you where I hate ; therefore beseech you
    To avert your liking a more worthier way
    Than on a wretch whom nature is asham'd
    Almost to acknowledge hers.
Fra.   This is most strange,
    That she, that even but now was your best object,
    The argument of your praise, balm of your age,
    Most best, most dearest, should in this trice of time
    Commit a thing so monstrous, to dismantle
    So many folds of favour. Sure, her offence   220
    Must be of such unnatural degree
    That monsters it, or your fore-vouch'd affections
    Fall'n into taint ; which to believe of her,
    Must be a faith that reason without miracle
    Could never plant in me.
Cord.   I yet beseech your majesty,—
    If for I want that glib and oily art,
    To speak and purpose not, since what I well intend,
    I 'll do 't before I speak,—that you make known
    It is no vicious blot, murder, or foulness,
    No unclean action, or dishonour'd step,   230
    That hath depriv'd me of your grace and favour ;
    But even for want of that for which I am rich,
    A still-soliciting eye, and such a tongue
    As I am glad I have not, though not to have it
    Hath lost me in your liking.
Lear.   Go to, go to. Better thou
    Hadst not been born than not to have pleas'd me
      better.
Fra. Is it no more but this, a tardiness in nature
    That often leaves the history unspoke
    That it intends to do ? My lord of Burgundy,
    What say you to the lady ? Love is not love   240
    When it is mingled with respects that stands
    Aloof from the entire point. Will you have her ?
    She is herself and dower.
Bur.   Royal Lear,

    Give but that portion which yourself propos'd,
    And here I take Cordelia by the hand,
    Duchess of Burgundy.
Lear. Nothing ; I have sworn.   {I am firm}
Bur. I am sorry then you have so lost a father
    That you must lose a husband.
Cord.   Peace be with Burgundy !
    Since that respects of fortune are his love,   250
    I shall not be his wife.
Fra. Fairest Cordelia, that art most rich being poor,
    Most choice forsaken, and most lov'd despis'd,
    Thee and thy virtues here I seize upon ;
    Be it lawful I take up what 's cast away.
    Gods, gods ! 'tis strange, that from their cold'st neglect
    My love should kindle to inflam'd respect.
    Thy dowerless daughter, king, thrown to my chance,
    Is queen of us, of ours, and our fair France :
    Not all the dukes in waterish Burgundy   260
    Shall buy this unpriz'd precious maid of me.
    Bid them farewell, Cordelia, though unkind :
    Thou losest here, a better where to find.
Lear. Thou hast her, France, let her be thine, for we
    Have no such daughter, nor shall ever see
    That face of hers again. Therefore be gone,
    Without our grace, our love, our benison.
    Come, noble Burgundy.
        Flourish. Exeunt all but France,
          Goneril, Regan, and Cordelia
Fra. Bid farewell to your sisters.
Cord. The jewels of our father, with wash'd eyes
    Cordelia leaves you : I know you what you are ;   271
    And, like a sister, am most loath to call
    Your faults as they are nam'd. Use well our father :
    To your professed bosoms I commit him :
    But yet, alas, stood I within his grace,
    I would prefer him to a better place.
    So farewell to you both.
Reg. Prescribe not us our duties.
Gon.   Let your study
    Be to content your lord, who hath receiv'd you
    At fortune's alms. You have obedience scanted,   280
    And well are worth the worth that you have wanted.
Cord. Time shall unfold what pleated cunning hides,
    Who covers faults, at last shame them derides.
    Well may you prosper !
Fra.   Come, fair Cordelia.
        Exeunt France and Cordelia
Gon. Sister, it is not a little I have to say of what most
    nearly appertains to us both. I think our father will
    hence to-night.
Reg. That 's most certain, and with you ; next month
    with us.
Gon. You see how full of changes his age is ; the observa-   290
    tion we have made of it hath not been little : he
    always loved our sister most ; and with what poor
    judgement he hath now cast her off appears too gross.
Reg. 'Tis the infirmity of his age : yet he hath ever but
    slenderly known himself.
Gon. The best and soundest of his time hath been but rash ;
    ·then must we look to receive from his age not alone
    the imperfection of long ingrafted condition, but
    therewithal unruly waywardness, that infirm and
    choleric years bring with them.   300
Reg. Such unconstant starts are we like to have from him
    as this of Kent's banishment.
Gon. There is further compliment of leave-taking between
    France and him. Pray let 's hit together : if our
    father carry authority with such dispositions as he
    bears, this last surrender of his will but offend us.
Reg. We shall further think on 't.
Gon. We must do something, and i' the heat.   *Exeunt*

SCENE II
The Earl of Gloucester's castle
Enter Edmund, with a letter

Edm. Thou, Nature, art my goddess ; to thy law
    My services are bound. Wherefore should I
    Stand in the plague of custom, and permit
    The curiosity of nations to deprive me,
    For that I am some twelve or fourteen moonshines
    Lag of a brother ? Why bastard ? wherefore base ?
    When my dimensions are as well compact,
    My mind as generous, and my shape as true,
    As honest madam's issue, why brand they us
    With base, base bastardy ?   10
    Who in the lusty stealth of nature take
    More composition and fierce quality
    Than doth within a stale, dull, tired bed,
    Go to the creating a whole tribe of fops,
    Got 'tween a sleep and wake. Well then,
    Legitimate Edgar, I must have your land :
    Our father's love is to the bastard Edmund,
    As to the legitimate : {fine word, ' legitimate ' :}
    Well, my legitimate, if this letter speed,
    And my invention thrive, Edmund the base   20
    Shall top the legitimate. I grow, I prosper,
    Now gods stand up for bastards !
        Enter Gloucester
Glo. Kent banish'd thus, and France in choler parted,
    And the king gone to-night, subscrib'd his power,
    Confin'd to exhibition ; all this done
    Upon the gad ! Edmund, how now, what news ?
Edm. So please your lordship, none.
        Putting up the letter
Glo. Why so earnestly seek you to put up that letter ?
Edm. I know no news, my lord.
Glo. What paper were you reading ?   30
Edm. Nothing, my lord.
Glo. No ? What needs then that terrible dispatch of it
    into your pocket ? the quality of nothing hath not
    such need to hide itself. Let 's see : come, if it be
    nothing, I shall not need spectacles.
Edm. I beseech you, sir, pardon me, it is a letter from my
    brother, that I have not all o'er-read ; for so much
    as I have perus'd, I find it not fit for your liking.
Glo. Give me the letter, sir.
Edm. I shall offend either to detain or give it ; the con-   40
    tents, as in part I understand them, are to blame.
Glo. Let 's see, let 's see.
Edm. I hope, for my brother's justification, he wrote this
    but as an essay, or taste of my virtue.
Glo. *(reads)* ' This policy {and reverence} of age makes
    the world bitter to the best of our times, keeps our
    fortunes from us till our oldness cannot relish them ;
    I begin to find an idle and fond bondage in the
    oppression of aged tyranny, who sways not as it hath
    power, but as it is suffer'd. Come to me, that of this   50
    I may speak more. If our father would sleep till I
    wak'd him, you should enjoy half his revenue for
    ever, and live the belov'd of your brother EDGAR.'
    Hum ! Conspiracy !—' slept till I wak'd him, you
    should enjoy half his revenue !'—My son Edgar !
    Had he a hand to write this, a heart and brain to
    breed it in ? When came this to you, who brought it ?
Edm. It was not brought me, my lord, there 's the
    cunning of it ; I found it thrown in at the casement   60
    of my closet.
Glo. You know the character to be your brother's ?
Edm. If the matter were good, my lord, I durst swear it
    were his, but, in respect of that, I would fain think
    it were not.

Glo. It is his ?

Edm. It is his hand, my lord, but I hope his heart is not in the contents.

Glo. Hath he never heretofore sounded you in this business ?   70

Edm. Never, my lord, but I have often heard him maintain it to be fit, that, sons at perfect age, and fathers declining, his father should be as ward to the son, and the son manage the revenue.

Glo. O villain, villain ! His very opinion in the letter ! Abhorred villain, unnatural, detested, brutish villain, worse than brutish ! Go, sir, seek him, ay, apprehend him, abominable villain ! Where is he ?

Edm. I do not well know, my lord. If it shall please you   80 to suspend your indignation against my brother till you can derive from him better testimony of this intent, you should run a certain course, where, if you violently proceed against him, mistaking his purpose, it would make a great gap in your own honour, and shake in pieces the heart of his obedience. I dare pawn down my life for him, he hath wrote this to feel my affection to your honour, and to no further pretence of danger.

Glo. Think you so ?   90

Edm. If your honour judge it meet, I will place you where you shall hear us confer of this, and by an auricular assurance have your satisfaction, and that without any further delay than this very evening.

Glo. He cannot be such a monster—

[*Edm.* Nor is not, sure.

Glo. To his father, that so tenderly and entirely loves him. Heaven and earth !] Edmund, seek him out, wind me into him, I pray you, frame your business after your own wisdom. I would unstate myself to be in   100 a due resolution.

Edm. I shall seek him, sir, presently, convey the business as I shall see means, and acquaint you withal.

Glo. These late eclipses in the sun and moon portend no good to us : though the wisdom of nature can reason thus and thus, yet nature finds itself scourg'd by the sequent effects : love cools, friendship falls off, brothers divide : in cities, mutinies ; in countries, discords ; in palaces, treason ; the bond crack'd between son and father. {This villain of mine   110 comes under the prediction ; there 's son against father : the king falls from bias of nature ; there 's father against child. We have seen the best of our time : machinations, hollowness, treachery and all ruinous disorders follow us disquietly to our graves.} Find out this villain, Edmund ; it shall lose thee nothing ; do it carefully. And the noble and true-hearted Kent banish'd ! his offence, honest ! Strange, strange !

            Exit

Edm. This is the excellent foppery of the world, that when   120 we are sick in fortune—often the surfeit of our own behaviour—we make guilty of our disasters the sun, the moon and the stars : as if we were villains by necessity, fools by heavenly compulsion, knaves, thieves and trecherers by spherical predominance, drunkards, liars and adulterers by an enforc'd obedience of planetary influence, and all that we are evil in, by a divine thrusting on : an admirable evasion of whoremaster man, to lay his goatish disposition to the charge of stars ! My father com-   130 pounded with my mother under the dragon's tail, and my nativity was under Ursa major ; so that it follows, I am rough and lecherous. Fut, I should have been that I am, had the maidenlest star of the firmament twinkled on my bastardy. [Edgar—]

Enter Edgar

And out he comes like the Catastrophe of the old comedy : my cue is villanous melancholy, with a sigh like Tom o' Bedlam. O, these eclipses do portend these divisions ! {fa, sol, la, mi.}

Edg. How now, brother Edmund ? what serious con-   140 templation are you in ?

Edm. I am thinking, brother, of a prediction I read this other day, what should follow these eclipses.

Edg. Do you busy yourself about that ?

Edm. I promise you, the effects he writ of succeed un-happily ; [as of unnaturalness between the child and the parent, death, dearth, dissolutions of ancient amities, divisions in state, menaces and maledic-tions against king and nobles, needless diffidences, banishment of friends, dissipation of cohorts, nuptial   150 breaches, and I know not what.

Edg. How long have you been a sectary astronomical ?

Edm. Come, come ;] when saw you my father last ?

Edg. Why, the night gone by.

Edm. Spake you with him ?

Edg. Two hours together.

Edm. Parted you in good terms ? Found you no dis-pleasure in him by word or countenance ?

Edg. None at all.

Edm. Bethink yourself wherein you may have offended   160 him, and at my entreaty forbear his presence till some little time hath qualified the heat of his dis-pleasure, which at this instant so rageth in him that with the mischief of your person it would scarcely allay.

Edg. Some villain hath done me wrong.

Edm. That 's my fear. {I pray you, have a continent forbearance till the speed of his rage goes slower, and, as I say, retire with me to my lodging, from whence I will fitly bring you to hear my lord speak :   170 pray ye, go ; there 's my key : if you do stir abroad, go arm'd.

Edg. Arm'd, brother !}

Edm. Brother, I advise you to the best : [go arm'd :] I am no honest man if there be any good meaning towards you : I have told you what I have seen and heard, but faintly, nothing like the image and horror of it : pray you, away !

Edg. Shall I hear from you anon ?

Edm. I do serve you in this business.   *Exit Edgar* 180 A credulous father, and a brother noble, Whose nature is so far from doing harms That he suspects none, on whose foolish honesty My practices ride easy, I see the business. Let me, if not by birth, have lands by wit : All with me 's meet that I can fashion fit.   *Exit*

SCENE III

The Duke of Albany's palace

Enter Goneril and Oswald, her steward

Gon. Did my father strike my gentleman for chiding of his fool ?

Osw. Yes, madam.

Gon. By day and night he wrongs me ; every hour He flashes into one gross crime or other, That sets us all at odds : I 'll not endure it : His knights grow riotous, and himself upbraids us On every trifle. When he returns from hunting, I will not speak with him ; say I am sick : If you come slack of former services,   10 You shall do well ; the fault of it I 'll answer.

Osw. He 's coming, madam, I hear him.   *Horns within*

Gon. Put on what weary negligence you please,

You and your fellow servants ; I 'ld have it come in question : If he dislike it, let him to our sister, Whose mind and mine, I know, in that are one, [Not to be over-rul'd. Idle old man, That still would manage those authorities That he hath given away ! Now, by my life, Old fools are babes again, and must be us'd   20 With checks as flatteries, when they are seen abus'd.] Remember what I tell you.

Osw.   Very well, madam.

Gon. And let his knights have colder looks among you ; What grows of it, no matter ; advise your fellows so : [I would breed from hence occasions, and I shall, That I may speak :] I 'll write straight to my sister, To hold my very course. Go, prepare for dinner.

           Exeunt

SCENE IV

A hall in the same

Enter Kent, disguised

Kent. If but as well I other accents borrow, That can my speech defuse, my good intent May carry through itself to that full issue For which I raz'd my likeness. Now, banish'd Kent, If thou canst serve where thou dost stand condemn'd, {So may it come,} thy master whom thou lovest Shall find thee full of labour.

 Horns within. Enter Lear, Knights, and Attendants

Lear. Let me not stay a jot for dinner ; go get it ready. *(exit an Attendant.)* How now, what art thou ?

Kent. A man, sir.   10

Lear. What dost thou profess ? What wouldst thou with us ?

Kent. I do profess to be no less than I seem, to serve him truly that will put me in trust, to love him that is honest, to converse with him that is wise and says little, to fear judgement, to fight when I cannot choose, and to eat no fish.

Lear. What art thou ?

Kent. A very honest-hearted fellow, and as poor as the king.

Lear. If thou be as poor for a subject as he is for a king,   20 thou art poor enough. What wouldst thou ?

Kent. Service.

Lear. Who wouldst thou serve ?

Kent. You.

Lear. Dost thou know me, fellow ?

Kent. No, sir ; but you have that in your countenance which I would fain call master.

Lear. What 's that ?

Kent. Authority.

Lear. What services canst do ?   30

Kent. I can keep honest counsel, ride, run, mar a curious tale in telling it, and deliver a plain message bluntly ; that which ordinary men are fit for, I am qualified in, and the best of me is diligence.

Lear. How old art thou ?

Kent. Not so young to love a woman for singing, nor so old to dote on her for any thing : I have years on my back forty eight.

Lear. Follow me, thou shalt serve me ; if I like thee no worse after dinner, I will not part from thee   40 yet. Dinner, ho, dinner ! Where 's my knave, my fool ? Go you and call my fool hither.

         Exit an Attendant

Enter Oswald

You, sirrah, where 's my daughter ?

Osw. So please you,—   *Exit*

Lear. What says the fellow there ? Call the clotpole back.

(*exit a Knight.*) Where 's my fool, ho? I think the world 's asleep.

Re-enter Knight

How now, where 's that mongrel?

Knt. He says, my lord, your daughter is not well.

Lear. Why came not the slave back to me when I call'd 50
him?

Kni. Sir, he answer'd me in the roundest manner, he would not.

Lear. 'A would not?

Kni. My lord, I know not what the matter is; but, to my judgement, your highness is not entertain'd with that ceremonious affection as you were wont; there 's a great abatement appears as well in the general dependants as in the duke himself also and your daughter. 60

Lear. Ha! sayest thou so?

Kni. I beseech you pardon me, my lord, if I be mistaken; for my duty cannot be silent when I think your highness wrong'd.

Lear. Thou but rememberest me of mine own conception: I have perceiv'd a most faint neglect of late; which I have rather blam'd as mine own jealous curiosity than as a very pretence and purport of unkindness: I will look further into 't. But where 's this fool? I have not seen him this two days. 70

Kni. Since my young lady 's going into France, sir, the fool hath much pin'd away.

Lear. No more of that, I have noted it. Go you and tell my daughter I would speak with her. (*exit an Attendant.*) Go you, call hither my fool.

Exit an Attendant

Re-enter Oswald

O, you sir, you sir, come you hither, who am I, sir?

Osw. My lady's father.

Lear. My lady's father? my lord's knave, you whoreson dog, you slave, you cur!

Osw. I am none of this, my lord, I beseech you pardon me. 80

Lear. Do you bandy looks with me, you rascal?

Striking him

Osw. I 'll not be struck, my lord.

Kent. Nor tripp'd neither, you base foot-ball player.

Tripping him up

Lear. I thank thee, fellow; thou serv'st me, and I 'll love thee.

Kent. Come, sir, I 'll teach you differences: away, away! If you will measure your lubber's length again, tarry: but away! {go to;} you have wisdom? {so.}

Pushes Oswald out

Lear. Now, friendly knave, I thank thee: there 's earnest of thy service. *Giving Kent money* 90

Enter Fool

Fool. Let me hire him too; here 's my coxcomb.

Offering Kent his cap

Lear. How now, my pretty knave, how dost thou?

Fool. Sirrah, you were best take my coxcomb.

Kent. Why, fool?

Fool. Why, for taking on 's part that 's out of favour: nay, an thou canst not smile as the wind sits, thou 'lt catch cold shortly; there, take my coxcomb; why, this fellow hath banished two on 's daughters, and done the third a blessing against his will; if thou follow him, thou must needs 100 wear my coxcomb. How now, nuncle? Would I had two coxcombs and two daughters!

Lear. Why, my boy?

Fool. If I gave them all my living, I 'ld keep my coxcombs myself. There 's mine; beg another of thy daughters.

Lear. Take heed, sirrah; the whip.

Fool. Truth is a dog that must to kennel, he must be whipp'd out, when Lady the brach may stand by the fire and stink. 110

Lear. A pestilent gall to me!

Fool. Sirrah, I 'll teach thee a speech.

Lear. Do.

Fool Mark it, uncle:

> Have more than thou showest,
> Speak less than thou knowest,
> Lend less than thou owest,
> Ride more than thou goest,
> Learn more than thou trowest,
> Set less than thou throwest; 120
> Leave thy drink and thy whore,
> And keep in-a-door,
> And thou shalt have more
> Than two tens to a score.

Kent. This is nothing, fool.

Fool. Then 'tis like the breath of an unfee'd lawyer, you gave me nothing for 't. Can you make no use of nothing, uncle?

Lear. Why, no, boy; nothing can be made out of nothing.

Fool. (*to Kent*) Prithee, tell him, so much the rent of his 130 land comes to; he will not believe a fool.

Lear. A bitter fool!

Fool. Dost know the difference, my boy, between a bitter fool and a sweet fool?

Lear. No, lad; teach me.

[*Fool.*   That lord that counsell'd thee
> To give away thy land,
> Come place him here by me;
> Do thou for him stand:
> The sweet and bitter fool 140
> Will presently appear;
> The one in motley here,
> The other found out there.

Lear. Dost thou call me fool, boy?

Fool. All thy other titles thou hast given away; that thou wast born with.

Kent. This is not altogether fool, my lord.

Fool. No, faith, lords and great men will not let me; if I had a monopoly on 't, they would have part on 't: and ladies too, they will not let me have all the fool 150 to myself; they 'll be snatching.] Give me an egg, nuncle, and I 'll give thee two crowns.

Lear. What two crowns shall they be?

Fool. Why, after I have cut the egg in the middle and eat up the meat, the two crowns of the egg; when thou clovest thy crown i' the middle and gavest away both parts, thou borest thine ass on thy back o'er the dirt: thou hadst little wit in thy bald crown when thou gavest thy golden one away. If I speak like myself in this, let him be whipp'd that 160 first finds it so.

(*singing*) Fools had ne'er less wit in a year;
> For wise men are grown foppish,
> They know not how their wits do wear,
> Their manners are so apish.

Lear. When were you wont to be so full of songs, sirrah?

Fool. I have us'd it, nuncle, ever since thou madest thy daughters thy mother: for when thou gavest them the rod and putst down thine own breeches,

(*singing*) Then they for sudden joy did weep, 170
> And I for sorrow sung,
> That such a king should play bo-peep,
> And go the fools among.

Prithee, nuncle, keep a schoolmaster that can teach thy fool to lie: I would fain learn to lie.

Lear. An you lie, we 'll have you whipp'd.

Fool. I marvel what kin thou and thy daughters are: they 'll have me whipp'd for speaking true, thou wilt have me whipp'd for lying, and sometime I am whipp'd for holding my peace; I had rather be 180 any kind of thing than a fool, and yet I would not be thee, nuncle; thou hast par'd thy wit a' both sides and left nothing in the middle. Here comes one of the parings.

Enter Goneril

Lear. How now, daughter, what makes that frontlet on? Methinks you are too much of late i' the frown.

Fool. Thou wast a pretty fellow when thou hadst no need to care for her frown; now thou art an O without a figure: I am better than thou art now; I am a fool, thou art nothing. Yes, forsooth, I will hold 190 my tongue; so your face bids me, though you say nothing.

Mum, mum:
> He that keeps neither crust nor crumb,
> Weary of all, shall want some.

(*pointing to Lear*) That 's a sheal'd peascod.

Gon. Not only, sir, this, your all-licens'd fool,
But other of your insolent retinue,
Do hourly carp and quarrel, breaking forth
In rank and not to be endured riots. Sir, 200
I had thought, by making this well known unto you,
To have found a safe redress, but now grow fearful,
By what yourself too late have spoke and done,
That you protect this course, and put it on
By your allowance; which if you should, the fault
Would not 'scape censure, nor the redress sleep,
Which, in the tender of a wholesome weal,
Might in their working do you that offence
That else were shame, that then necessity
Must call discreet proceeding. 210

Fool. For, you know, nuncle,
> The hedge-sparrow fed the cuckoo so long,
> That it had it head bit off by it young.

So out went the candle, and we were left darkling.

Lear. Are you our daughter?

Gon. Come, sir,
I would you would make use of that good wisdom
Whereof I know you are fraught, and put away
These dispositions that of late transform you
From what you rightly are. 220

Fool. May not an ass know when the cart draws the horse? Whoop, Jug, I love thee.

Lear. Doth any here know me? Why, this is not Lear:
Doth Lear walk thus? speak thus? Where are his eyes?
Either his notion weakens, his discernings
Are lethargied—Ha! waking? 'tis not so.
Who is it that can tell me who I am?

Fool. Lear's shadow.

[*Lear.* I would learn that; for, by the marks of sovereignty, knowledge and reason, I should be false 230
persuaded I had daughters.]

Fool. Which they will make an obedient father.]

Lear. Your name, fair gentlewoman?

Gon. Come, sir!
This admiration is much o' the savour
Of other your new pranks. I do beseech
You understand my purposes aright;
As you are old and reverend, should be wise.
Here do you keep a hundred knights and squires,
Men so disorder'd, so debosh'd and bold, 240
That this our court, infected with their manners,
Shows like a riotous inn: epicurism and lust
Make it more like a tavern or brothel
Than a great palace. The shame itself doth speak
For instant remedy: be thou desir'd
By her, that else will take the thing she begs,
A little to disquantity your train,
And the remainder that shall still depend,

    To be such men as may besort your age,
    That know themselves and you.
Lear.   Darkness, and devils !   250
    Saddle my horses, call my train together.
    Degenerate bastard, I 'll not trouble thee :
    Yet have I left a daughter.
Gon. You strike my people, and your disorder'd rabble
    Make servants of their betters.

               Enter Albany

Lear. We, that too late repent 's,— (*to Alb.*) [O, sir, are
    you come ?]
    Is it your will that we— Prepare my horses.
    Ingratitude, thou marble-hearted fiend,
    More hideous when thou show'st thee in a child
    Than the sea-monster !
{*Alb.*   Pray, sir, be patient.}   260
Lear. (*to Gon.*) Detested kite ! thou liest.
    My train are men of choice and rarest parts,
    That all particulars of duty know,
    And in the most exact regard support
    The worships of their name. O most small fault,
    How ugly didst thou in Cordelia show !
    That, like an engine, wrench'd my frame of nature
    From the fix'd place, drew from my heart all love
    And added to the gall. O Lear, Lear,
    Beat at this gate, that let thy folly in   270

               Striking his head

    And thy dear judgement out ! Go, go, my people,
Alb. My lord, I am guiltless, as I am ignorant
    {Of what hath mov'd you.}
Lear.   It may be so, my lord.
    Hark, Nature, hear, dear goddess !
    Suspend thy purpose, if thou didst intend
    To make this creature fruitful ;
    Into her womb convey sterility,
    Dry up in her the organs of increase,
    And from her derogate body never spring
    A babe to honour her ! If she must teem,   280
    Create her child of spleen, that it may live
    And be a thwart disfeatur'd torment to her,
    Let it stamp wrinkles in her brow of youth,
    With cadent tears fret channels in her cheeks,
    Turn all her mother's pains and benefits
    To laughter and contempt, that she may feel
    How sharper than a serpent's tooth it is
    To have a thankless child ! Go, go, my people ! *Exit*
Alb. Now, gods that we adore, whereof comes this ?
Gon. Never afflict yourself to know the cause,   290
    But let his disposition have that scope
    That dotage gives it.

               Re-enter Lear

Lear. What, fifty of my followers at a clap,
    Within a fortnight !
Alb.   What is the matter, sir ?
Lear. I 'll tell thee. (*to Gon.*) Life and death ! I am
    asham'd
    That thou hast power to shake my manhood thus,
    That these hot tears, that break from me perforce,
    Should make thee worth them. Blasts and fogs
    upon thee !
    The untented woundings of a father's curse
    Pierce every sense about thee ! Old fond eyes,   300
    Beweep this cause again, I 'll pluck you out
    And cast you with the waters that you make
    To temper clay ; [yea, is 't come to this ?] {ha, let it
    be so !}
    Yet have I left a daughter,
    Who I am sure is kind and comfortable :
    When she shall hear this of thee, with her nails
    She 'll flay thy wolvish visage. Thou shalt find
    That I 'll resume the shape which thou dost think

    I have cast off for ever : thou shalt, I warrant thee.

           Exeunt Lear, Kent, and Attendants

Gon. Do you mark that, my lord ?   310
Alb. I cannot be so partial, Goneril,
    To the great love I bear you,—
Gon. Come, sir, no more.
    (*to the Fool*) You, more knave than fool, after your
    master.
Fool. Nuncle Lear, nuncle Lear, tarry and take the fool, with
    A fox, when one has caught her,
    And such a daughter,
    Should sure to the slaughter,
    If my cap would buy a halter :
    So the fool follows after.   *Exit* 320
{*Gon.* This man hath had good counsel : a hundred
    knights !
    'Tis politic and safe to let him keep
    At point a hundred knights : yes, that on every dream,
    Each buzz, each fancy, each complaint, dislike,
    He may enguard his dotage with their powers
    And hold our lives in mercy. Oswald, I say !
Alb. Well, you may fear too far.
Gon.   Safer than trust too far :
    Let me still take away the harms I fear,
    Not fear still to be taken : I know his heart.
    What he hath utter'd I have writ my sister :   330
    If she sustain him and his hundred knights,
    When I have show'd the unfitness,—}
Gon. What, Oswald, ho !
Osw. Here, Madam.
Gon. What, have you writ this letter to my sister ?
Osw. Yes, madam.
Gon. Take you some company, and away to horse,
    Inform her full of my particular fears,
    And thereto add such reasons of your own
    As may compact it more. Get you gone ;   340
    And hasten your return. (*exit Oswald.*) Now, my
    lord,
    This milky gentleness and course of yours
    Though I dislike not, yet, under pardon,
    You are much more attask'd for want of wisdom
    Than prais'd for harmful mildness.
Alb. How far your eyes may pierce I cannot tell :
    Striving to better, oft we mar what 's well.
Gon. Nay, then—
Alb. Well, well ; the events.   *Exeunt*

SCENE V

Court before the same

Enter Lear, Kent, and Fool

Lear. Go you before to Gloucester with these letters.
    Acquaint my daughter no further with any thing you
    know than comes from her demand out of the letter.
    If your diligence be not speedy, I shall be there before
    you.
Kent. I will not sleep, my lord, till I have delivered your
    letter.   *Exit*
Fool. If a man's brains were in 's heels, were 't not in
    danger of kibes ?
Lear. Ay, boy.   10
Fool. Then I prithee be merry, thy wit shall ne'er go
    slip-shod.
Lear. Ha, ha, ha !
Fool. Shalt see thy other daughter will use thee kindly,
    for though she 's as like this as a crab is like an
    apple, yet I con what I can tell.
Lear. Why, what canst thou tell, my boy ?
Fool. She 'll taste as like this as a crab doth to a crab ;
    thou canst not tell why one's nose stands i' the
    middle of his face ?   20

Lear. No.
Fool. Why, to keep his eyes on either side 's nose, that
    what a man cannot smell out 'a may spy into.
Lear. I did her wrong—
Fool. Canst tell how an oyster makes his shell ?
Lear. No.
Fool. Nor I neither, but I can tell why a snail has a
    house.
Lear. Why ?
Fool. Why, to put his head in, not to give it away to   30
    his daughters, and leave his horns without a case.
Lear. I will forget my nature.—So kind a father !—Be
    my horses ready ?
Fool. Thy asses are gone about them ; the reason why
    the seven stars are no more than seven is a pretty
    reason.
Lear. Because they are not eight ?
Fool. Yes, thou wouldst make a good fool.
Lear. To take 't again perforce ! Monster, ingratitude !
Fool. If thou wert my fool, nuncle, I 'ld have thee beaten   40
    for being old before thy time.
Lear. How 's that ?
Fool. Thou shouldst not have been old before thou hadst
    been wise.
Lear. O, let me not be mad, I would not be mad ; sweet
    heaven !
    Keep me in temper : I would not be mad !

             Enter Gentleman

    Are the horses ready ?
Gent. Ready, my lord.
Lear. Come, boy.
Fool. She that is a maid now, and laughs at my departure   50
    Shall not be a maid long, except things be cut
    shorter.   *Exeunt*

Act Second

SCENE I

The Earl of Gloucester's castle

Enter Edmund and Curan, meeting

Edm. Save thee, Curan.
Cur. And you, sir. I have been with your father, and
    given him notice that the Duke of Cornwall and
    his duchess will be here with him to-night.
Edm. How comes that ?
Cur. Nay, I know not. You have heard of the news
    abroad, I mean the whisper'd ones, for they are yet
    but ear-bussing arguments ?
Edm. Not I : pray you, what are they ?
Cur. Have you heard of no likely wars towards, twixt   10
    the two Dukes of Cornwall and Albany ?
Edm. Not a word.
Cur. You may then in time. Fare you well, sir.   *Exit*
Edm. The duke be here to-night ? The better best ;
    This weaves itself perforce into my business.
    My father hath set guard to take my brother,
    And I have one thing of a queasy question,
    Which must ask briefness and fortune's help.
    Brother, a word ; descend, brother, I say !

             Enter Edgar

    My father watches : O fly this place ;   20
    Intelligence is given where you are hid ;
    You have now the good advantage of the night :
    Have you not spoken 'gainst the Duke of Cornwall
    ought ?
    He 's coming hither now i' the night, i' the haste,
    And Regan with him : have you nothing said
    Upon his party against the Duke of Albany ?
    Advise your—

Edg.   I am sure on 't, not a word.
Edm. I hear my father coming : pardon me :
          In cunning I must draw my sword upon you,
          Seem to defend. yourself, now quit you well.   30
          Yield : come before my father.   Light, here, here !
          Fly, brother, fly !   Torches, torches !   So farewell.
                                                        Exit Edgar
          Some blood drawn on me would beget opinion
                                                Wounds his arm
          Of my more fierce endeavour : I have seen drunkards
          Do more than this in sport.   Father, father !
          Stop, stop !   No help ?
                Enter Gloucester, and Servants with torches
Glo. Now, Edmund, where is the villain ?
Edm. Here stood he in the dark, his sharp sword out,
          Warbling of wicked charms, conjuring the moon
          To stand 's auspicious mistress.
Glo.   But where is he ?   40
Edm. Look, sir, I bleed.
Glo.   Where is the villain, Edmund ?
Edm. Fled this way, sir.   When by no means he could—
Glo. Pursue him—Go after.   (*exeunt some Servants.*)   ' By
          no means ' what ?
Edm. Persuade me to the murder of your lordship ;
          But that I told him the revengive gods
          'Gainst parricides did all their thunders bend,
          Spoke with how manifold and strong a bond
          The child was bound to the father ; sir, in fine,
          Seeing how loathly opposite I stood
          To his unnatural purpose, with fell motion   50
          With his prepared sword he charges home
          My unprovided body, lanc'd mine arm :
          But when he saw my best alarum'd spirits
          Bold in the quarrel's rights, rous'd to the encounter,
          Or whether gasted by the noise I made,
          But suddenly he fled.
Glo.   Let him fly far :
          Not in this land shall he remain uncaught,
          And found—dispatch.   The noble duke my master,
          My worthy arch and patron, comes to-night ;
          By his authority I will proclaim it,   60
          That he which finds him shall deserve our thanks,
          Bringing the murderous caitiff to the stake ;
          He that conceals him, death.
Edm. When I dissuaded him from his intent
          And found him pight to do it, with curst speech
          I threaten'd to discover him ; he replied,
          ' Thou unpossessing bastard ! dost thou think,
          If I would stand against thee, could the reposure
          Of any trust, virtue, or worth, in thee
          Make thy words faith'd ?   No : what I should deny—   70
          As this I would, ay, though thou didst produce
          My very character—I 'ld turn it all
          To thy suggestion, plot, and damned pretence,
          And thou must make a dullard of the world,
          If they not thought the profits of my death
          Were very pregnant and potential spurs
          To make thee seek it.'
Glo.   Strong and fasten'd villain !
          Would he deny his letter ?   I never got him.
                                                Tucket within
          Hark, the duke's trumpets !   I know not why he
             comes.
          All ports I 'll bar, the villain shall not 'scape,   80
          The duke must grant me that : besides, his picture
          I will send far and near, that all the kingdom
          May have note of him ; and of my land,
          Loyal and natural boy, I 'll work the means
          To make thee capable.
              Enter Cornwall, Regan, and Attendants
Corn. How now, my noble friend ?   since I came hither,

          Which I can call but now, I have heard strange news.
Reg. If it be true, all vengeance comes too short
          Which can pursue the offender.   How dost, my lord ?
Glo. Madam, my old heart is crack'd, is crack'd !   90
Reg. What, did my father's godson seek your life ?
          He whom my father nam'd, your Edgar ?
Glo. Ay, lady, lady, shame would have it hid !
Reg. Was he not companion with the riotous knights
          That tend upon my father ?
Glo. I know not, madam : 'tis too bad, too bad.
Edm. Yes, madam, he was {of that consort.}
Reg. No marvel then, though he were ill affected :
          'Tis they have put him on the old man's death,
          To have the expense and waste of his revenues.   100
          I have this present evening from my sister
          Been well inform'd of them, and with such cautions
          That if they come to sojourn at my house,
          I 'll not be there.
Corn.   Nor I, assure thee, Regan.
          Edmund, I hear that you have shown your father
          A child-like office.
Edm.   'Twas my duty, sir.
Glo. He did betray his practice, and receiv'd
          This hurt you see, striving to apprehend him.
Corn. Is he pursued ?
Glo.   Ay, my good lord.
Corn. If he be taken, he shall never more   110
          Be fear'd of doing harm : make your own purpose,
          How in my strength you please.   For you, Edmund,
          Whose virtue and obedience doth this instant
          So much commend itself, you shall be ours :
          Natures of such deep trust we shall much need :
          You we first seize on.
Edm.   I shall serve you,
          Truly, however else.
Glo.   For him I thank your grace.
Corn. You know not why we came to visit you,—
Reg. Thus out of season, threading dark-eyed night ;
          Occasions, noble Gloucester, of some poise,   120
          Wherein we must have use of your advice :
          Our father he hath writ, so hath our sister,
          Of differences, which I best thought it fit
          To answer from our home ; the several messengers
          From hence attend dispatch.   Our good old friend,
          Lay comforts to your bosom, and bestow
          Your needful counsel to our business,
          Which craves the instant use.
Glo.   I serve you, madam :
          Your graces are right welcome.   *Exeunt*

                              SCENE II

                      Before Gloucester's castle

                  Enter Kent and Oswald, severally

Osw. Good even to thee, friend, art of the house ?
Kent. Ay.
Osw. Where may we set our horses ?
Kent. I' the mire.
Osw. Prithee, if thou love me, tell me.
Kent. I love thee not.
Osw. Why then I care not for thee.
Kent. If I had thee in Lipsbury pinfold, I would make thee
          care for me.
Osw. Why dost thou use me thus ?   I know thee not.   10
Kent. Fellow, I know thee.
Osw. What dost thou know me for ?
Kent. A knave, a rascal, an eater of broken meats, a base,
          proud, shallow, beggarly, three-suited, hundred-
          pound, filthy, worsted-stocking knave, a lily-liver'd
          action-taking knave, a whoreson glass-gazing super-

serviceable finical rogue, one trunk-inheriting slave,
          one that wouldst be a bawd in way of good service,
          and art nothing but the composition of a knave,
          beggar, coward, pandar, and the son and heir of   20
          a mongrel bitch, whom I will beat into clamorous
          whining, if thou deny the least syllable of the
          addition.
Osw. What a monstrous fellow art thou, thus to rail on
          one that 's neither known of thee nor knows thee !
Kent. What a brazen-fac'd varlet art thou, to deny thou
          knowest me !   Is it two days ago since I beat thee
          and tripp'd up thy heels before the king ?   Draw,
          you rogue, for, though it be night, the moon shines ;
          I 'll make a sop o' the moonshine a' you : draw, you
          whoreson cullionly barber-monger, draw !   31
                                          Drawing his sword
Osw. Away !   I have nothing to do with thee.
Kent. Draw, you rascal : you bring letters against the king,
          and take Vanity the puppet's part against the royalty
          of her father : draw, you rogue, or I 'll so carbonado
          your shanks—draw, you rascal, come your ways.
Osw. Help, ho !   murder !   help !
Kent. Strike, you slave, stand, rogue, stand, you neat
          slave, strike !   *Beating him*
Osw. Help, ho !   murder !   help !   40

            *Enter Edmund, with his rapier drawn, Cornwall, Regan,
                      Gloucester, and Servants*

Edm. How now, what 's the matter ?   *Parting them*
Kent. With you, goodman boy, an you please come, I 'll
          flesh you ; come on, young master.
Glo. Weapons ? arms ?   What 's the matter here ?
Corn. Keep peace, upon your lives ;
          He dies that strikes again.   What 's the matter ?
Reg. The messengers from our sister and the king.
Corn. What 's your difference ?   speak.
Osw. I am scarce in breath, my lord.
Kent. No marvel, you have so bestirr'd your valour.   You   50
          cowardly rascal, nature disclaims in thee, a tailor
          made thee.
Corn. Thou art a strange fellow : a tailor make a man ?
Kent. Ay, a tailor, sir ; a stone-cutter or a painter could not
          have made him so ill, though he had been but two
          hours at the trade.
Corn. Speak yet, how grew your quarrel ?
Osw. This ancient ruffian, sir, whose life I have spar'd at
          suit of his gray beard,—
Kent. Thou whoreson zed, thou unnecessary letter !   My   60
          lord, if you 'll give me leave, I will tread this un-
          bolted villain into mortar, and daub the walls of a
          jakes with him.   Spare my gray beard, you wagtail ?
Corn. Peace, sir !
          You beastly knave, have you no reverence ?
Kent. Yes, sir ; but anger has a privilege.
Corn. Why art thou angry ?
Kent. That such a slave as this should wear a sword,
          Who wears no honesty.   Such smiling rogues as these,
          Like rats, oft bite those cords a-twain which are   70
          Too intrinse to unloose ; smooth every passion
          That in the natures of their lords rebel ;
          Bring oil to fire, snow to their colder moods,
          Renege, affirm, and turn their halcyon beaks
          With every gale and vary of their masters,
          Knowing nought, like dogs, but following.
          A plague upon your epileptic visage !
          Smoile you my speeches, as I were a fool ?
          Goose, an I had you upon Sarum plain,
          I 'ld send you cackling home to Camelot.
Corn. What, art thou mad, old fellow ?   81
Glo. How fell you out ?   say that.
Kent. No contraries hold more antipathy

Than I and such a knave.

Corn. Why dost thou call him knave ? What 's his offence ?

Kent. His countenance likes me not.

Corn. No more perchance does mine, nor his, nor hers.

Kent. Sir, 'tis my occupation to be plain :
  I have seen better faces in my time
  Than stands on any shoulder that I see   90
  Before me at this instant.

Corn.   This is a fellow,
  Who, having been prais'd for bluntness, doth affect
  A saucy roughness, and constrains the garb
  Quite from his nature : he cannot flatter, he,
  He must be plain, he must speak truth !
  An they will take it, so ; if not, he 's plain.
  These kind of knaves I know, which in this plainness
  Harbour more craft and more corrupter ends
  Than twenty silly ducking observants
  That stretch their duties nicely.   100

Kent. Sir, ' in good sooth,' or ' in sincere verity,'
  ' Under the allowance of your grand aspect,
  Whose influence, like the wreath of radiant fire
  On flickering Phœbus' front,'—

Corn.   What mean'st thou by this ?

Kent. To go out of my dialect, which you discommend
  so much. I know, sir, I am no flatterer : he that
  beguil'd you in a plain accent was a plain knave ;
  which, for my part, I will not be, though I should
  win your displeasure to entreat me to 't.

Corn. What 's the offence you gave him ?   110

Osw. I never gave him any :
  It pleas'd the king his master very late
  To strike at me, upon his misconstruction,
  When he, conjunct, and flattering his displeasure,
  Tripp'd me behind ; being down, insulted, rail'd,
  And put upon him such a deal of man,
  That worthied him, got praises of the king
  For him attempting who was self-subdued,
  And in the fleshment of this dread exploit
  Drew on me here again.

Kent.   None of these rogues and cowards 120
  But Ajax is their fool.

Corn.   Bring forth the stocks ho !
  You stubborn ancient knave, you reverend braggart,
  We 'll teach you—

Kent.   I am too old to learn :
  Call not your stocks for me : I serve the king,
  On whose employments I was sent to you :
  You should do small respect, show too bold malice
  Against the grace and person of my master,
  Stocking his messenger.

Coru. Fetch forth the stocks !   As I have life and honour,
  There he shall sit till noon.   130

Reg. Till noon ! till night, my lord, and all night too.

Kent. Why, madam, if I were your father's dog,
  You could not use me so.

Reg.   Sir, being his knave, I will.

Corn. This is a fellow of the self-same nature
  Our sister speaks of. Come, bring away the stocks !
                    Stocks brought out

Glo. Let me beseech your grace not to do so :
  [His fault is much, and the good king his master
  Will check him for 't : your purposed low correction
  Is such as basest and contemned'st wretches
  For pilferings and most common trespasses   140
  Are punish'd with :] the king must take it ill,
  That he 's so slightly valued in his messenger,
  Should have him thus restrain'd.

Corn.   I 'll answer that.

Reg. My sister may receive it much more worse,
  To have her gentlemen abus'd, assaulted,
  [For following her affairs. Put in his legs.]
                    Kent is put in the stocks

Come, my good lord, away.
                    Exeunt all but Gloucester and Kent

Glo. I am sorry for thee, friend, 'tis the duke's pleasure,
  Whose disposition, all the world well knows,
  Will not be rubb'd nor stopp'd : I 'll entreat for thee.

Kent. Pray you, do not, sir : I have watch'd and travell'd
  hard ;   151
  Some time I shall sleep out, the rest I 'll whistle.
  A good man's fortune may grow out at heels :
  Give you good morrow !

Glo. The duke 's to blame in this, 'twill be ill took.
                    Exit

Kent. Good king, that must approve the common saw,
  Thou out of heaven's benediction comest
  To the warm sun !
  Approach, thou beacon to this under globe,
  That by thy comfortable beams I may   160
  Peruse this letter ! Nothing almost sees miracles
  But misery : I know 'tis from Cordelia,
  Who hath most fortunately been inform'd
  Of my obscured course ; and shall find time
  From this enormous state, seeking to give
  Losses their remedies. All weary and o'er-watch'd,
  Take vantage, heavy eyes, not to behold
  This shameful lodging.
  Fortune, good night : smile ; once more turn thy
  wheel !   *Sleeps*

SCENE III

A wood

Enter Edgar

Edg. I heard myself proclaim'd ;
  And by the happy hollow of a tree
  Escap'd the hunt. No port is free, no place,
  That guard and most unusual vigilance
  Does not attend my taking. While I may 'scape
  I will preserve myself, and am bethought
  To take the basest and most poorest shape
  That ever penury in contempt of man
  Brought near to beast ; my face I 'll grime with filth,
  Blanket my loins, elf all my hair with knots,   10
  And with presented nakedness out-face
  The wind and persecution of the sky.
  The country gives me proof and precedent
  Of Bedlam beggars, who with roaring voices
  Strike in their numb'd and mortified bare arms
  Pins, wooden pricks, nails, sprigs of rosemary ;
  And with this horrible object, from low farms,
  Poor pelting villages, sheep-cotes and mills,
  Sometime with lunatic bans, sometime with prayers,
  Enforce their charity. Poor Turlygod ! poor Tom ! 20
  That 's something yet : Edgar I nothing am. *Exit*

SCENE IV

Before Gloucester's castle. Kent in the stocks

Enter Lear, Fool, and Gentleman

Lear. 'Tis strange that they should so depart from home,
  And not send back my messenger.

Gent.   As I learn'd,
  The night before there was no purpose in them
  Of this remove.

Kent.   Hail to thee, noble master !

Lear. How ?
  Makest thou this shame thy pastime ?

{*Kent.*   No, my lord}

Fool. Ha, ha ! Look, he wears crewel garters. Horses are
tied by the heads, dogs and bears by the neck,
monkeys by the loins, and men by the legs ; when
a man's over-lusty at legs, then he wears wooden   10
nether-stocks.

Lear. What 's he that hath so much thy place mistook
  To set thee here ?

Kent.   It is both he and she,
  Your son and daughter.

Lear. No.

Kent. Yes.

Lear. No, I say.

Kent. I say yea.

[*Lear.* No, no, they would not.

Kent. Yes, they have.]   20

Lear. By Jupiter, I swear, no.

{*Kent.* By Juno, I swear, ay.}

Lear.   They durst not do 't ;
  They would not, could not do 't, 'tis worse than
  murder,
  To do upon respect such violent outrage :
  Resolve me with all modest haste, which way
  Thou may'st deserve, or they impose, this usage,
  Coming from us.

Kent.   My lord, when at their home
  I did commend your highness' letters to them,
  Ere I was risen from the place that show'd
  My duty kneeling, came there a reeking post,   30
  Stew'd in his haste, half breathless, panting forth
  From Goneril his mistress salutations ;
  Deliver'd letters, spite of intermission,
  Which presently they read ; on whose contents
  They summon'd up their meiny, straight took horse,
  Commanded me to follow, and attend
  The leisure of their answer, gave me cold looks,
  And meeting here the other messenger,
  Whose welcome, I perceiv'd, had poison'd mine—
  Being the very fellow that of late   40
  Display'd so saucily against your highness—
  Having more man than wit about me, drew :
  He rais'd the house with loud and coward cries.
  Your son and daughter found this trespass worth
  This shame which here it suffers.

{*Fool.* Winter 's not gone yet, if the wild geese fly that way.
            Fathers that wear rags
                Do make their children blind ;
            But fathers that bear bags
                Shall set their children kind.   50
            Fortune, that arrant whore,
            Ne'er turns the key to the poor.
  But, for all this, thou shalt have as many dolours
  for thy daughters as thou canst tell in a year.}

Lear. O, how this mother swells up toward my heart !
  Hysterica passio, down, thou climbing sorrow,
  Thy element 's below ! Where is this daughter ?

Kent. With the earl, sir, within.

Lear. Follow me not, stay there.   *Exit*

Gent. Made you no more offence than what you speak of ? 60

Kent. No.
  How chance the king comes with so small a train ?

Fool. An thou hadst been set i' the stocks for that question,
thou hadst well deserved it.

Kent. Why, fool ?

Fool. We 'll set thee to school to an ant, to teach thee
there 's no labouring in the winter. All that follow
their noses are led by their eyes but blind men ; and
there 's not a nose among a hundred but can smell him
that 's stinking. Let go thy hold when a great wheel   70
runs down a hill, lest it break thy neck with following
it ; but the great one that goes up the hill, let him
draw thee after. When a wise man gives thee better
counsel, give me mine again : I would have none but

knaves follow it, since a fool gives it.
    That sir that serves for gain,
      And follows but for form,
    Will pack when it begins to rain,
      And leave thee in the storm.
    But I will tarry, the fool will stay,   80
      And let the wise man fly :
    The knave turns fool that runs away :
      The fool no knave, perdy.
Kent. Where learned you this, fool ?
Fool. Not i' the stocks.
          Re-enter Lear, with Gloucester
Lear. Deny to speak with me ? They 're sick ? they 're
    weary ?
    They travell'd hard to-night ? Mere fetches ; ay,
    The images of revolt and flying off.
    Fetch me a better answer.
Glo.   My dear lord,
    You know the fiery quality of the duke ;   90
    How unremoveable and fix'd he is
    In his own course.
Lear. Vengeance, death, plague, confusion !
    What fiery quality ? Why, Gloucester, Gloucester,
    I 'ld speak with the Duke of Cornwall, and his wife.
{*Glo.* Well, my good lord, I have inform'd them so.
Lear. Inform'd them ! Dost thou understand me, man ?}
Glo. Ay, my good lord.
Lear. The king would speak with Cornwall ; the dear
    father   99
    Would with his daughter speak, commands her service :
    {Are they inform'd of this ? My breath and blood !}
    ' Fiery duke ' ? Tell the hot duke that Lear—
    No, but not yet ; may be he is not well ;
    Infirmity doth still neglect all office
    Whereto our health is bound ; we are not ourselves
    When nature being oppress'd commands the mind
    To suffer with the body : I 'll forbear,
    And am fall'n out with my more headier will,
    To take the indispos'd and sickly fit
    For the sound man. Death on my state ! wherefore   110
    Should he sit here ? This act persuades me
    That this remotion of the duke and her
    Is practice only. Give me my servant forth.
    Go tell the duke and 's wife I 'll speak with them,
    Now, presently ; bid them come forth and hear
    me,
    Or at their chamber-door I 'll beat the drum
    Till it cry sleep to death.
Glo. I would have all well betwixt you.   *Exit*
Lear. O my heart, my heart !
Fool. Cry to it, nuncle, as the cockney did to the eels when   120
    she put 'em i' the paste alive ; she rapp'd 'em o'
    the coxcombs with a stick, and cried ' Down, wantons,
    down !' 'Twas her brother that, in pure kindness
    to his horse, buttered his hay.

    Re-enter Gloucester, with Cornwall, Regan, and Servants
Lear. Good morrow to you both.
Corn.   Hail to your grace !
                   Kent is set at liberty
Reg. I am glad to see your highness.
Lear. Regan, I think you are ; I know what reason
    I have to think so ; if thou shouldst not be glad,
    I would divorce me from thy mother's tomb,
    Sepulchring an adultress. (*to Kent*) Yea, are you free ?   130
    Some other time for that. Beloved Regan,
    Thy sister is naught, O Regan, she hath tied
    Sharp-tooth'd unkindness, like a vulture, here :
                       Points to his heart
    I can scarce speak to thee, thou 'lt not believe
    With how depriv'd a quality—O Regan !
Reg. I pray, sir, take patience : I have hope

You less know how to value her desert
    Than she to slack her duty.
{*Lear.*   Say, how is that ?
Reg. I cannot think my sister in the least
    Would fail her obligation : if, sir, perchance   140
    She have restrain'd the riots of your followers,
    'Tis on such ground and to such wholesome end
    As clears her from all blame.}
Lear. My curses on her !
Reg.   O, sir, you are old ;
    Nature in you stands on the very verge
    Of her confine ; you should be rul'd and led
    By some discretion that discerns your state
    Better than you yourself. Therefore I pray
    That to our sister you do make return ;
    Say you have wrong'd her, sir.
Lear.   Ask her forgiveness ?   150
    Do you mark how this becomes the house :
    (*kneeling*) ' Dear daughter, I confess that I am old,
    Age is unnecessary, on my knees I beg
    That you 'll vouchsafe me raiment, bed and food.'
Reg. Good sir, no more ; these are unsightly tricks :
    Return you to my sister.
Lear.   (*rising*) No, Regan :
    She hath abated me of half my train,
    Look'd black upon me, struck me with her tongue,
    Most serpent-like, upon the very heart :
    All the stor'd vengeances of heaven fall   160
    On her ingrateful top ! Strike her young bones,
    You taking airs, with lameness.
Corn.   Fie, fie, sir !
Lear. You nimble lightnings, dart your blinding flames
    Into her scornful eyes, infect her beauty,
    You fen-suck'd fogs, drawn by the powerful sun,
    To fall and blast her pride.
Reg. O the blest gods ! so will you wish on me,
    When the rash mood . . .
Lear. No, Regan, thou shalt never have my curse :
    Thy tender-hefted nature shall not give
    Thee o'er to harshness ; her eyes are fierce, but thine   171
    Do comfort and not burn. 'Tis not in thee
    To grudge my pleasures, to cut off my train,
    To bandy hasty words, to scant my sizes,
    And, in conclusion, to oppose the bolt
    Against my coming in ; thou better know'st
    The offices of nature, bond of childhood,
    Effects of courtesy, dues of gratitude ;
    Thy half o' the kingdom hast thou not forgot,
    Wherein I thee endow'd.
Reg.   Good sir, to the purpose.   180
Lear. Who put my man i' the stocks ?   *Tucket within*
Corn.   What trumpet 's that ?
Reg. I know 't my sister's : this approves her letters,
    That she would soon be here.
               Enter Oswald
             Is your lady come ?
Lear. This is a slave whose easy-borrow'd pride
    Dwells in the fickle grace of her he follows.
    Out, varlet, from my sight !
Corn.   What means your grace ?

            Enter Goneril
Gon. Who struck my servant ? Regan, I have good hope
    Thou didst not know on 't.
Lear.   Who comes here ? O heavens,
    If you do love old men, if your sweet sway
    Allow obedience, if yourselves are old,   190
    Make it your cause ; send down, and take my part !
    (*to Gon.*) Art not asham'd to look upon this beard ?
    O Regan, wilt thou take her by the hand ?
Gon. Why not by the hand, sir ? How have I offended ?
    All 's not offence that indiscretion finds

And dotage terms so.
Lear.   O sides, you are too tough,
    Will you yet hold ? How came my man i' the stocks ?
Corn. I set him there, sir, but his own disorders
    Deserv'd much less advancement.
Lear.   You, did you ?
Reg. I pray you, father, being weak, seem so.   200
    If, till the expiration of your month,
    You will return and sojourn with my sister,
    Dismissing half your train, come then to me :
    I am now from home and out of that provision
    Which shall be needful for your entertainment.
Lear. Return to her, and fifty men dismiss'd ?
    No, rather I abjure all roofs, and choose
    To wage against the enmity o' the air,
    To be a comrade with the wolf and owl,—
    Necessity's sharp pinch ! Return with her ?   210
    Why, the hot-blood in France, that dowerless took
    Our youngest born, I could as well be brought
    To knee his throne, and, squire-like, pension beg
    To keep base life afoot. Return with her ?
    Persuade me rather to be slave and sumpter
    To this detested groom.   *Pointing at Oswald*
Gon.   At your choice, sir.
Lear. Now, I prithee, daughter, do not make me mad ;
    I will not trouble thee, my child ; farewell :
    We 'll no more meet, no more see one another :
    But yet thou art my flesh, my blood, my daughter,   220
    Or rather a disease that lies within my flesh,
    Which I must needs call mine ; thou art a boil,
    A plague-sore, an embossed carbuncle,
    In my corrupted blood. But I 'll not chide thee ;
    Let shame come when it will, I do not call it :
    I do not bid the thunder-bearer shoot,
    Nor tell tales of thee to high-judging Jove :
    Mend when thou canst, be better at thy leisure ;
    I can be patient, I can stay with Regan,
    I and my hundred knights.
Reg.   Not altogether so, sir :   230
    I look'd not for you yet, nor am provided
    For your fit welcome. Give ear, sir, to my sister ;
    For those that mingle reason with your passion
    Must be content to think you are old, and so—
    But she knows what she does.
Lear.   Is this well spoken now ?
Reg.   I dare avouch it, sir : what, fifty followers ?
    Is it not well ? What should you need of more ?
    Yea, or so many, sith that both charge and danger
    Speak 'gainst so great a number ? How in a house
    Should many people under two commands   240
    Hold amity ? 'Tis hard, almost impossible.
Gon. Why might not you, my lord, receive attendance
    From those that she calls servants, or from mine ?
Reg. Why not, my lord ? If then they chanc'd to slack you.
    We could control them. If you will come to me,
    For now I spy a danger, I entreat you
    To bring but five and twenty, to no more
    Will I give place or notice.
Lear. I gave you all—
Reg.   And in good time you gave it.
Lear. Made you my guardians, my depositaries,   250
    But kept a reservation to be follow'd
    With such a number. What, must I come to you
    With five and twenty ; Regan, said you so ?
Reg. And speak 't again, my lord, no more with me.
Lear. Those wicked creatures yet do look well-favour'd,
    When others are more wicked ; not being the worst
    Stands in some rank of praise. (*to Gon.*) I 'll go with
    thee,
    Thy fifty yet doth double five and twenty,
    And thou art twice her love.

Gon.   Hear me, my lord :
What need you five and twenty, ten, or five,   260
To follow in a house where twice so many
Have a command to tend you ?
Reg.   What needs one ?
*Lear.*O, reason not the need : our basest beggars
Are in the poorest thing superfluous :
Allow not nature more than nature needs,
Man's life 's as cheap as beast's : thou art a lady ;
If only to go warm were gorgeous,
Why, nature needs not what thou gorgeous wear'st,
Which scarcely keeps thee warm. But for true need,—
You heavens, give me that patience, patience I need !   270
You see me here, you gods, a poor old fellow,
As full of grief as age, wretched in both :
If it be you that stirs these daughters' hearts
Against their father, fool me not too much
To bear it tamely ; touch me with noble anger,
And let not women's weapons, water-drops,
Stain my man's cheeks ! No, you unnatural hags,
I will have such revenges on you both
That all the world shall—I will do such things,—
What they are, yet I know not, but they shall be   280
The terrors of the earth. You think I 'll weep ;
No, I 'll not weep : I have full cause of weeping,
                 Storm and tempest
But this heart shall break in a hundred thousand flaws,
Or ere I 'll weep. O fool, I shall go mad !
       Exeunt Lear, Gloucester, Kent, and Fool
*Corn.*Let us withdraw ; 'twill be a storm.
Reg. This house is little, the old man and his people
Cannot be well bestow'd.
Gon. 'Tis his own blame hath put himself from rest,
And must needs taste his folly.
Reg. For his particular, I 'll receive him gladly,   290
But not one follower.
Gon.   So am I purposed.
Where is my lord of Gloucester ?
*Corn.*Follow'd the old man forth : he is return'd.
            Re-enter Gloucester
Glo. The king is in high rage.
{*Corn.*   Whither is he going ?
Glo. He calls to horse ;} and will I know not whither.
Corn.'Tis good to give him way ; he leads himself.
Gon. My lord, entreat him by no means to stay.
Glo. Alack, the night comes on, and the bleak winds
Do sorely ruffle ; for many miles about
There 's not a bush.
Reg.   O, sir, to wilful men   300
The injuries that they themselves procure
Must be their schoolmasters ; shut up your doors :
He is attended with a desperate train,
And what they may incense him to, being apt
To have his ear abus'd, wisdom bids fear.
*Corn.*Shut up your doors, my lord, 'tis a wild night ;
My Regan counsels well, come out o' the storm.
                     Exeunt

Act Third

SCENES I AND II

A heath

Storm still. Enter Kent and a Gentleman, meeting

*Kent.*What 's here, beside foul weather ?
*Gent.*One minded like the weather, most unquietly.
*Kent.*I know you ; where 's the king ?

---

*Gent.*Contending with the fretful element ;
Bids the wind blow the earth into the sea,
Or swell the curled waters 'bove the main,
That things might change or cease ; [tears his white
     hair,
Which the impetuous blasts, with eyeless rage,
Catch in their fury, and make nothing of ;
Strives in his little world of man to out-scorn   10
The to-and-fro-conflicting wind and rain.
This night, wherein the cub-drawn bear would couch,
The lion, and the belly-pinched wolf,
Keep their fur dry, unbonneted he runs,
And bids what will take all.]
Kent.   But who is with him ?
*Gent.*None but the fool, who labours to out-jest
His heart-struck injuries.
Kent.   Sir, I do know you,
And dare, upon the warrant of my note,
Commend a dear thing to you. There is division,   20
Although as yet the face of it be cover'd
With mutual cunning, 'twixt Albany and Cornwall ;
{Who have—as who have not, that their great stars
Throned and set high ?—servants, who seem no less,
Which are to France the spies and speculations
Intelligent of our state ; what hath been seen,
Either in snuffs and packings of the dukes,
Or the hard rein which both of them have borne
Against the old kind king, or something deeper,
Whereof perchance these are but furnishings,—}
[But true it is, from France there comes a power   30
Into this scatter'd kingdom, who already,
Wise in our negligence, have secret feet
In some of our best ports, and are at point
To show their open banner. Now to you ;
If on my credit you dare build so far
To make your speed to Dover, you shall find
Some that will thank you, making just report
Of how unnatural and bemadding sorrow
The king hath cause to plain.
I am a gentleman of blood and breeding,   40
And from some knowledge and assurance offer
This office to you.]
*Gent.*I will talk farther with you.
Kent.   No, do not.
For confirmation that I am much more
Than my out-wall, open this purse and take
What it contains. If you shall see Cordelia,—
As fear not but you shall,—show her this ring,
And she will tell you who your fellow is
That yet you do not know. Fie on this storm !
I will go seek the king.
Gent.   Give me your hand :   50
Have you no more to say ?
*Kent.*Few words, but to effect more than all yet ;
That, when we have found the king,
I 'll this way, you that,—he that first lights on him
Holla the other.   *Exeunt severally*

         Enter Lear and Fool

*Lear.*Blow, winds, and crack your cheeks ! rage ! blow !
You cataracts and hurricanoes, spout
Till you have drench'd the steeples, drown'd the cocks !
You sulphurous and thought-executing fires,
Vaunt-couriers to oak-cleaving thunderbolts,
Singe my white head ! And thou, all-shaking thunder,
Smite flat the thick rotundity o' the world,
Crack nature's mould, all germins spill at once
That make ingrateful man !
*Fool.*O nuncle, court holy-water in a dry house is better   10
than this rain-water out o' door. Good nuncle, in,
and ask thy daughters' blessing ; here 's a night pities
neither wise man nor fool.

---

*Lear.*Rumble thy bellyful ! Spit, fire ! spout, rain !
Nor rain, wind, thunder, fire, are my daughters :
I tax not you, you elements, with unkindness,
I never gave you kingdom, call'd you children,
You owe me no subscription : why then, let fall
Your horrible pleasure ; here I stand, your slave,
A poor, infirm, weak and despis'd old man ;   20
But yet I call you servile ministers,
That have with two pernicious daughters join'd
Your high-engender'd battle 'gainst a head
So old and white as this. O ! 'tis foul !
*Fool.*He that has a house to put his head in has a good
head-piece.
     The cod-piece that will house
       Before the head has any,
     The head and he shall louse
       So beggars marry many.   30
     The man that makes his toe
       What he his heart should make
     Shall of a corn cry woe,
       And turn his sleep to wake.
For there was never yet fair woman but she made
mouths in a glass.
*Lear.*No, I will be the pattern of all patience ;
I will say nothing.
             Enter Kent
*Kent.*Who 's there ?
*Fool.*Marry, here 's grace and a cod-piece ; that 's a wise   40
man and a fool.
*Kent.*Alas, sir, sit you here ? things that love night
Love not such nights as these ; the wrathful skies
Gallow the very wanderers of the dark,
And make them keep their caves : since I was man,
Such sheets of fire, such bursts of horrid thunder,
Such groans of roaring wind and rain, I ne'er
Remember to have heard : man's nature cannot carry
The afflictions nor the force.
Lear.   Let the great gods,
That keep this dreadful pother o'er our heads,   50
Find out their enemies now. Tremble, thou wretch,
That hast within thee undivulged crimes,
Unwhipp'd of justice : hide thee, thou bloody hand,
Thou perjur'd, and thou simular man of virtue
That art incestuous : caitiff, in pieces shake,
That under covert and convenient seeming
Hast practis'd on man's life : close pent-up guilts,
Rive your concealed centres and cry
These dreadful summoners grace. I am a man
More sinn'd against than sinning.
Kent.   Alack, bare-headed !   60
Gracious my lord, hard by here is a hovel ;
Some friendship will it lend you 'gainst the tempest :
Repose you there, whilst I to this hard house—
More hard than is the stone whereof 'tis rais'd ;
Which even but now, demanding after you,
Denied me to come in—return, and force
Their scanted courtesy.
Lear.   My wit begins to turn.
Come on, my boy : how dost, my boy ? art cold ?
I am cold myself ; where is this straw, my fellow ?
The art of our necessities is strange,   70
That can make vile things precious. Come, your
hovel.
Poor fool and knave, I have one part in my heart
That sorrows yet for thee.
Fool.(*singing*)
     He that has a little tiny wit,—
       With hey, ho, the wind and the rain,—
     Must make content with his fortunes fit,
     For the rain it raineth every day.
*Lear.*True, my good boy. Come, bring us to this hovel.
            Exeunt Lear and Kent

{*Fool.*This is a brave night to cool a courtezan.
    I 'll speak a prophecy ere I go :   80
        When priests are more in word than matter ;
        When brewers mar their malt with water ;
        When nobles are their tailors' tutors ;
        No heretics burn'd, but wenches' suitors ;
        When every case in law is right ;
        No squire in debt, nor no poor knight ;
        When slanders do not live in tongues,
        Nor cutpurses come not to throngs ;
        When usurers tell their gold i' the field,
        And bawds and whores do churches build,   90
        Then shall the realm of Albion
        Come to great confusion :
        Then comes the time, who lives to see 't,
        That going shall be used with feet.
    This prophecy Merlin shall make ; for I live before
    his time.   *Exit*}

SCENE III

Gloucester's castle

Enter Gloucester and Edmund, with lights

Glo. Alack, alack, Edmund, I like not this unnatural
dealing. When I desired their leave that I might
pity him, they took from me the use of mine own
house, charg'd me, on pain of their displeasure,
neither to speak of him, entreat for him, nor any
way sustain him.

*Edm.*Most savage and unnatural !

Glo. Go to, say you nothing. There's a division
betwixt the dukes, and a worse matter than that,
I have receiv'd a letter this night ; 'tis dangerous   10
to be spoken ; I have lock'd the letter in my closet :
these injuries the king now bears will be revenged
home ; there's part of a power already landed ; we
must incline to the king. I will seek him and privily
relieve him : go you, and maintain talk with the
duke, that my charity be not of him perceived : if he
ask for me, I am ill and gone to bed. Though I die
for it, as no less is threaten'd me, the king my old
master must be relieved. There is some strange
thing toward ; Edmund, pray you, be careful.   20
                                 Exit

*Edm.*This courtesy, forbid thee, shall the duke
Instantly know, and of that letter too :
This seems a fair deserving, and must draw me
That which my father loses ; no less than all :
Then younger rises when the old doth fall.   *Exit*

SCENE IV

The heath. Before a hovel

Enter Lear, Kent, and Fool

*Kent.*Here is the place, my lord, good my lord, enter :
    The tyranny of the open night 's too rough
    For nature to endure.   *Storm still*

Lear.   Let me alone.

*Kent.*Good my lord, enter.

Lear.   Wilt break my heart ?

*Kent.*I had rather break mine own. Good my lord, enter.

*Lear.*Thou think'st 'tis much that this contentious storm
    Invades us to the skin : so 'tis to thee ;
    But where the greater malady is fix'd
    The lesser is scarce felt. Thou 'ldst shun a bear,
    But if the flight lay toward the raging sea   10
    Thou 'ldst meet the bear i' the mouth. When the
        mind 's free

The body 's delicate : this tempest in my mind
Doth from my senses take all feeling else
Save what beats there. Filial ingratitude !
Is it not as this mouth should tear this hand
For lifting food to 't ? But I will punish sure.
No, I will weep no more. {In such a night
To shut me out ! Pour on ; I will endure.}
In such a night as this ! O Regan, Goneril !
Your old kind father, whose frank heart gave you
    all,—   20
O, that way madness lies, let me shun that ;
No more of that.

Kent.   Good my lord, enter.

*Lear.*Prithee, go in thyself, seek thine own ease :
    This tempest will not give me leave to ponder
    On things would hurt me more. But I 'll go in.
    {(*to the Fool*) In boy ; go first. You houseless
        poverty,—
    Nay, get thee in. I 'll pray, and then I 'll sleep.}
                              Fool goes in
    Poor naked wretches, wheresoe'er you are,
    That bide the pelting of this pitiless night,
    How shall your houseless heads, and unfed sides,   30
    Your loop'd and window'd raggedness, defend you
    From seasons such as these ? O, I have ta'en
    Too little care of this ! Take physic, pomp,
    Expose thyself to feel what wretches feel,
    That thou mayst shake the superflux to them
    And show the heavens more just.

{*Edg.* (*within*) Fathom and half, fathom and half !
    Poor Tom !   *The Fool runs out from the hovel*}

*Fool.*Come not in here, nuncle, here 's a spirit.
    Help me, help me !   40

*Kent.*Give me thy hand, who 's there ?

*Fool.*A spirit, he says his name 's poor Tom.

*Kent.*What art thou that dost grumble there i' the straw ?
    Come forth.

Enter Edgar disguised as a madman

Edg. Away ! the foul fiend follows me !
    ' Thorough the sharp hawthorn blows the cold wind.'
    Go to thy cold bed and warm thee.

*Lear.*Hast thou given all to thy two daughters, and art
    thou come to this ?

Edg. Who gives any thing to poor Tom ? whom the foul   50
fiend hath led through fire and through ford and
whirlpool, o'er bog and quagmire, that has laid
knives under his pillow, and halters in his pew, set
ratsbane by his pottage, made him proud of heart, to
ride on a bay trotting-horse over four-inch'd bridges,
to course his own shadow for a traitor. Bless thy
five wits ! Tom 's a-cold. Bless thee from whirl-
winds, star-blasting, and taking ! Do poor Tom
some charity, whom the foul fiend vexes. There
could I have him now, and there, and there   60
again.   *Storm still*

*Lear.*What, his daughters brought him to this pass ;
    Couldst thou save nothing ? Didst thou give them
    all ?

*Fool.*Nay, he reserv'd a blanket, else we had been all
    sham'd.

*Lear.*Now, all the plagues that in the pendulous air
    Hang fated o'er men's faults light on thy daughters !

*Kent.*He hath no daughters, sir.

*Lear.*Death, traitor ! nothing could have subdued nature   70
    To such a lowness but his unkind daughters ;
    Is it the fashion that discarded fathers
    Should have thus little mercy on their flesh ?
    Judicious punishment ! 'twas this flesh begot
    Those pelican daughters.

Edg.   Pilicock sat on Pelicocks hill :
        A, lo, lo, lo !

*Fool.*This cold night will turn us all to fools and madmen.

Edg. Take heed o' the foul fiend, obey thy parents, keep
    thy words justly, swear not, commit not with man's   80
    sworn spouse, set not thy sweet heart on proud
    array ; Tom 's a-cold.

*Lear.*What hast thou been ?

Edg. A serving-man, proud in heart and mind ; that curl'd
my hair, wore gloves in my cap, serv'd the lust of
my mistress' heart, and did the act of darkness with
her, swore as many oaths as I spake words, and broke
them in the sweet face of heaven ; one that slept in
the contriving of lust and wak'd to do it : wine lov'd   90
I deeply, dice dearly, and in woman out-paramour'd
the Turk : false of heart, light of ear, bloody of hand,
hog in sloth, fox in stealth, wolf in greediness, dog
in madness, lion in prey. Let not the creaking of
shoes, nor the rustling of silks, betray thy poor heart
to women ; keep thy foot out of brothel, thy hand
out of placket, thy pen from lender's book, and defy
the foul fiend.
    ' Still through the hawthorn blows the cold wind.'
    Hay, no, nonny.   100
    Dolphin my boy, my boy, sessa ! let him trot by.
                             Storm still

*Lear.*Why, thou wert better in thy grave than to answer
with thy uncovered body this extremity of the skies.
Is man no more but this ? Consider him well. Thou
owest the worm no silk, the beast no hide, the sheep
no wool, the cat no perfume. Here 's three on 's
are sophisticated ; thou art the thing itself : unaccommodated man is no more but such a poor, bare,
forked animal as thou art. Off, off, you lendings !
come on, be true !   *Tearing off his clothes*

*Fool.*Prithee, nuncle, be content ; 'tis a naughty night to   111
swim in. Now a little fire in a wild field were like
an old lecher's heart, a small spark, all the rest in 's
body cold. Look, here comes a walking fire.

Enter Gloucester, with a torch

Edg. This is the foul fiend Fliberdigibbet : he begins at
curfew, and walks till the first cock ; he gives the
web, and the pin, squinies the eye, and makes the
hare-lip, mildews the white wheat, and hurts the poor
creature of earth.
      Saint Withold footed thrice the 'old ;   120
      He met the night-mare and her nine-fold ;
          Bid her alight,
          And her troth plight,
      And aroint thee, witch, aroint thee !

*Kent.*How fares your grace ?

*Lear.*What 's he ?

*Kent.*Who 's there ? What is 't you seek ?

Glo. What are you there ? Your names ?

Edg. Poor Tom, that eats the swimming frog, the toad, the
todpole, the wall-newt, and the water, that in the   130
fury of his heart, when the foul fiend rages, eats cow-
dung for sallets, swallows the old rat and the ditch-
dog, drinks the green mantle of the standing pool,
who is whipp'd from tithing to tithing, and stock-
punished, and imprisoned, who hath had three suits
to his back, six shirts to his body, horse to ride and
weapon to wear ;
      But mice and rats and such small deer
      Have been Tom's food for seven long year.
    Beware my follower. Peace, Smolkin ; peace, thou
    fiend !   140

Glo. What, hath your grace no better company ?

Edg. The prince of darkness is a gentleman : Modu he 's
call'd, and Maho.

Glo. Our flesh and blood is grown so vile, my lord,
That it doth hate what gets it.

Edg. Poor Tom 's a-cold.

Glo. Go in with me : my duty cannot suffer
    To obey in all your daughters' hard commands :
    Though their injunction be to bar my doors,
    And let this tyrannous night take hold upon you,   150
    Yet have I ventur'd to come seek you out,
    And bring you where both food and fire is ready.
Lear. First let me talk with this philosopher.
    What is the cause of thunder ?
Kent. Good my lord, take his offer, go into the house.
Lear. I 'll talk a word with this most learned Theban.
    What is your study ?
Edg. How to prevent the fiend, and to kill vermin.
Lear. Let me ask you one word in private.
Kent. Importune him to go, my lord ;   160
    His wits begin to unsettle.
Glo.   Canst thou blame him ?
                        Storm still
    His daughters seek his death :. O, that good Kent !
    He said it would be thus, poor banish'd man !
    Thou say'st the king grows mad ; I 'll tell thee, friend,
    I am almost mad myself : I had a son,
    Now outlaw'd from my blood ; he sought my life,
    But lately, very late : I lov'd him, friend,
    No father his son dearer : true to tell thee,
    The grief hath craz'd my wits. What a night 's this !
    I do beseech your grace,—
Lear.   O, cry you mercy ;   170
    Noble philosopher, your company.
Edg. Tom 's a-cold.
Glo. In, fellow, there, into the hovel : keep thee warm.
Lear. Come, let 's in all.
Kent.   This way, my lord.
Lear.   With him ;
    I will keep still with my philosopher.
Kent. Good, my lord, soothe him ; let him take the fellow.
Glo. Take him you on.
Kent. Sirrah, come on ; go along with us.
Lear. Come, good Athenian.
Glo. No words, no words : hush.   180
Edg. Childe Rowland to the dark toun came :
    His word was still ' Fie, foh, and fum,
    I smell the blood of a British man.'   *Exeunt*

SCENE V

Gloucester's castle

Enter Cornwall and Edmund

Corn. I will have my revenge ere I depart the house.
Edm. How, my lord, I may be censured, that nature thus
    gives way to loyalty, something fears me to think of.
Corn. I now perceive, it was not altogether your brother's
    evil disposition made him seek his death, but a
    provoking merit, set a-work by a reproveable badness
    in himself.
Edm. How malicious is my fortune, that I must repent
    to be just ! This is the letter he spoke of, which
    approves him an intelligent party to the advantages   10
    of France. O heavens ! that his treason were not,
    or not I the detector !
Corn. Go with me to the duchess.
Edm. If the matter of this paper be certain, you have
    mighty business in hand.
Corn. True or false, it hath made thee earl of Gloucester.
    Seek out where thy father is, that he may be ready
    for our apprehension.
Edm. (*aside*) If I find him comforting the king, it will
    stuff his suspicion more fully.—I will persever in my   20
    course of loyalty, though the conflict be sore between
    that and my blood.
Corn. I will lay trust upon thee, and thou shalt find a
    dearer father in my love.   *Exeunt*

SCENE VI

A chamber in a farmhouse adjoining the castle

Enter Gloucester, Lear, Kent, Fool, and Edgar

Glo. Here is better than the open air ; take it thankfully ;
    I will piece out the comfort with what addition I
    can ; I will not be long from you.
Kent. All the power of his wits have given way to im-
    patience : the gods deserve your kindness.
                       Exit Gloucester
Edg. Frateretto calls me, and tells me Nero is an angler
    in the lake of darkness. Pray, innocent, beware the
    foul fiend.
Fool. Prithee, nuncle, tell me whether a madman be a
    gentleman or a yeoman.   10
Lear. A king, a king !
{*Fool.* No, he 's a yeoman that has a gentleman to his
    son, for he 's a mad yeoman that sees his son a
    gentleman before him.}
Lear. To have a thousand with red burning spits
    Come hissing in upon them,—
[*Edg.* The foul fiend bites my back.
Fool. He 's mad that trusts in the tameness of a wolf, a
    horse's health, a boy's love, or a whore's oath.
Lear. It shall be done, I will arraign them straight ;   20
    (*to Edgar*) Come, sit thou here, most learned justice ;
    (*to the Fool*) Thou, sapient sir, sit here. No, you she
        foxes . . .
Edg. Look where he stands and glares ! Wantest thou
    eyes at trial, madam ?
        Come o'er the bourn, Bessy, to me.
Fool.   Her boat hath a leak,
        And she must not speak
    Why she dares not come over to thee.
Edg. The foul fiend haunts poor Tom in the voice of a   30
    nightingale. Hoberdidance cries in Tom's belly
    for two white herring. Croak not, black angel ; I
    have no food for thee.
Kent. How do you, sir ? Stand you not so amaz'd :
    Will you lie down and rest upon the cushions ?
Lear. I 'll see their trial first. Bring in the evidence.
    (*to Edgar*) Thou robed man of justice, take thy place ;
    (*to the Fool*) And thou, his yoke-fellow of equity,
    Bench by his side. (*to Kent*) You are o' the com-
        mission ;   40
    Sit you too.
Edg. Let us deal justly.
        Sleepest or wakest thou, jolly shepherd ?
          Thy sheep be in the corn ;
        And for one blast of thy minikin mouth,
          Thy sheep shall take no harm.
    Pur the cat is gray.
Lear. Arraign her first ; 'tis Goneril. I here take my
    oath before this honourable assembly, kick'd the
    poor king her father.   50
Fool. Come hither, mistress. Is your name Goneril ?
Lear. She cannot deny it.
Fool. Cry you mercy, I took you for a joint-stool.
Lear. And here 's another, whose warp'd looks proclaim
    What store her heart is made on. Stop her there !
    Arms, arms, sword, fire ! Corruption in the place !
    False justicer, why hast thou let her 'scape ?]
Edg. Bless thy five wits !
Kent. O pity, sir ! Where is the patience now,
    That you so oft have boasted to retain ?   60
Edg. (*aside*) My tears begin to take his part so much,
    They 'll mar my counterfeiting.
Lear. The little dogs and all,
    Trey, Blanch, and Sweet-heart, see, they bark at me.
Edg. Tom will throw his head at them. Avaunt, you curs !
    Be thy mouth or black or white,
    Tooth that poisons if it bite ;
    Mastiff, greyhound, mongrel, grim,
    Hound or spaniel, brach or him,
    Bobtail tike or trundle-tail,   70
    Tom will make them weep and wail :
    For, with throwing thus my head,
    Dogs leap the hatch, and all are fled.
    Loudla, doodla ! Come, march to wakes and fairs
    and market-towns. Poor Tom, thy horn is dry.
Lear. Then let them anatomize Regan ; see what breeds
    about her heart. Is there any cause in nature that
    makes this hardness ? (*to Edgar*) You, sir, I enter-
    tain you for one of my hundred, only I do not like
    the fashion of your garments. You 'll say they are   80
    Persian attire, but let them be changed.
Kent. Now, good my lord, lie here awhile.
Lear. Make no noise, make no noise ; draw the curtains :
    so, so, so. We 'll go to supper i' the morning. So,
    so, so.
{*Fool.* And I 'll go to bed at noon.}
                    Re-enter Gloucester
Glo. Come hither, friend : where is the king my master ?
Kent. Here, sir, but trouble him not ; his wits are gone.
Glo. Good friend, I prithee, take him in thy arms ;
    I have o'erheard a plot of death upon him :   90
    There is a litter ready, lay him in 't,
    And drive towards Dover, friend, where thou shalt
        meet
    Both welcome and protection. Take up thy master :
    If thou shouldst dally half an hour, his life,
    With thine and all that offer to defend him,
    Stand in assured loss. Take up, take up,
    And follow me, that will to some provision
    Give thee quick conduct.
[*Kent.*   Oppressed nature sleeps.
    This rest might yet have balm'd thy broken sinews,
    Which, if convenience will not allow,   100
    Stand in hard cure. (*to the Fool*) Come, help to bear
        thy master ;
    Thou must not stay behind.]
Glo.   Come, come, away.
                  Exeunt [all but Edgar]
[*Edg.* When we our betters see bearing our woes,
    We scarcely think our miseries our foes.
    Who alone suffers suffers most i' the mind,
    Leaving free things and happy shows behind :
    But then the mind much sufferance doth o'erskip,
    When grief hath mates, and bearing fellowship.
    How light and portable my pain seems now,
    When that which makes me bend makes the king bow,
    He childed as I father'd ! Tom, away !   111
    Mark the high noises, and thyself bewray,
    When false opinion, whose wrong thoughts defile thee,
    In thy just proof repeals and reconciles thee.
    What will hap more to-night, safe 'scape the king !
    Lurk, lurk.]   *Exit*

SCENE VII

Gloucester's castle

Enter Cornwall, Regan, Goneril, Edmund, and Servants

Corn. Post speedily to my lord your husband ; show him
    this letter : the army of France is landed. Seek out
    the villain Gloucester.   *Exeunt some of the Servants*
Reg. Hang him instantly.
Gon. Pluck out his eyes.
Corn. Leave him to my displeasure. Edmund, keep you
    our sister company : the revenge we are bound to

take upon your traitorous father are not fit for your
beholding.   Advise the duke, where you are going,
to a most festinant preparation : we are bound to   10
the like.   Our post shall be swift and intelligence
betwixt us.   Farewell, dear sister : farewell, my lord
of Gloucester.
                    Enter Oswald
How now, where 's the king ?
Osw. My lord of Gloucester hath convey'd him hence :
Some five or six and thirty of his knights,
Hot questrists after him, met him at gate ;
Who, with some other of the lords dependants,
Are gone with him towards Dover, where they
          boast
To have well-armed friends.
Corn.   Get horses for your mistress.   20
Gon. Farewell, sweet lord, and sister.
Corn. Edmund, farewell.
               Exeunt Goneril, Edmund, and Oswald
Go seek the traitor Gloucester.
Pinion him like a thief, bring him before us.
                    Exeunt other Servants
Though we may not pass upon his life
Without the form of justice, yet our power
Shall do a courtesy to our wrath, which men
May blame but not control.   Who 's there ? the
          traitor ?
          Enter Gloucester, brought in by two or three
Reg. Ingrateful fox ! 'tis he.
Corn. Bind fast his corky arms.
Glo. What means your graces ?   Good my friends,
          consider   30
You are my guests : do me no foul play, friends.
Corn. Bind him, I say.   *Servants bind him*
Reg.   Hard, hard.   O filthy traitor !
Glo. Unmerciful lady as you are, I am true.
Corn. To this chair bind him.   Villain, thou shalt find—
                    Regan plucks his beard
Glo. By the kind gods, 'tis most ignobly done
To pluck me by the beard.
Reg. So white, and such a traitor !
Glo.   Naughty lady,
These hairs which thou dost ravish from my chin
Will quicken and accuse thee : I am your host :
With robbers' hands my hospitable favours   40
You should not ruffle thus.   What will you do ?
Corn. Come, sir, what letters had you late from France ?
Reg. Be simple answerer, for we know the truth.
Corn. And what confederacy have you with the traitors
Late footed in the kingdom ?
Reg. To whose hands you have sent the lunatic king :
Speak !
Glo. I have a letter guessingly set down,
Which came from one that 's of a neutral heart,
And not from one opposed.
Corn.   Cunning.
Reg.   And false.   50
Corn. Where hast thou sent the king ?
Glo.   To Dover.
Reg. Wherefore to Dover ?   Wast thou not charg'd at peril—
Corn. Wherefore to Dover ?   Let him first answer that.
Glo. I am tied to the stake, and I must stand the course.
Reg. Wherefore to Dover, sir ?
Glo. Because I would not see thy cruel nails
Pluck out his poor old eyes, nor thy fierce sister
In his anointed flesh rash boarish fangs.
The sea, with such a storm as his low'd head
In hell-black night endured, would have boil'd up,   60
And quench'd the stelled fires :
Yet, poor old heart, he holpt the heavens to rage ;
If wolves had at thy gate howl'd that derne time,

Thou shouldst have said, ' Good porter, turn the key,'
All cruels else subscrib'd : but I shall see   †
The winged vengeance overtake such children.
Corn. See 't shalt thou never.   Fellows, hold the chair.
Upon these eyes of thine I 'll set my foot.
Glo. He that will think to live till he be old,
Give me some help !   O cruel !   O ye gods !   70
Reg. One side will mock another ; t'other too.
Corn. If you see vengeance—
1.S.   Hold your hand, my lord :
I have serv'd you ever since I was a child ;
But better service have I never done you
Than now to bid you hold.
Reg.   How now, you dog !
1.S. If you did wear a beard upon your chin,
I 'ld shake it on this quarrel.   What do you mean ?
Corn. My villain !   *They draw and fight*
1.S. Why, then, come on, and take the chance of anger.
Reg. Give me thy sword.   A peasant stand up thus !   80
          Takes a sword and runs at him behind
1.S. O, I am slain, my lord ; yet have you one eye left
To see some mischief on him.   O !   *Dies*
Corn. Lest it see more, prevent it.   Out, vile jelly !
Where is thy lustre now ?
Glo. All dark and comfortless.   Where 's my son Edmund !
Edmund, enkindle all the sparks of nature,
To quit this horrid act.
Reg.   Out, villain !
Thou call'st on him that hates thee : it was he
That made the overture of thy treasons to us,
Who is too good to pity thee.   90
Glo. O my follies !   Then Edgar was abus'd.
Kind gods, forgive me that, and prosper him !
Reg. Go thrust him out at gates, and let him smell
His way to Dover.   *(exit one with Gloucester.)*   How
is 't, my lord ? how look you ?
Corn. I have receiv'd a hurt ; follow me, lady.
Turn out that eyeless villain, throw this slave
Upon the dunghill.   Regan, I bleed apace ;
Untimely comes this hurt, give me your arm.
                    Exit Cornwall, led by Regan
[*2.S.* I 'll never care what wickedness I do,
If this man come to good.
3.S.   If she live long,   100
And in the end meet the old course of death,
Women will all turn monsters,
2.S. Let 's follow the old earl, and get the Bedlam
To lead him where he would : his roguish madness
Allows itself to any thing.
3.S. Go thou : I 'll fetch some flax and whites of eggs
To apply to his bleeding face.   Now, heaven help
him !   *Exeunt severally*]

Act Fourth

SCENE I

The heath

Enter Edgar

Edg. Yet better thus, and known to be contemn'd,
Than still contemn'd and flatter'd to be worst ;
The lowest and most dejected thing of fortune,
Stands still in esperance, lives not in fear :
The lamentable change is from the best :
The worst returns to laughter.   {Welcome then,
Thou unsubstantial air that I embrace !
The wretch that thou hast blown unto the worst
Owes nothing to thy blasts.   But who comes here ?}

                    Enter Gloucester, led by an Old Man
                              Who 's here
My father, poorly led ?   World, world, O world !   10
But that thy strange mutations make us hate thee,
Life would not yield to age.
O.M. O, my good lord, I have been your tenant, and
your father's tenant, this four-score . . .
Glo. Away, get thee away ; good friend, be gone :
Thy comforts can do me no good at all,
Thee they may hurt.
O.M. Alack, sir, you cannot see your way.
Glo. I have no way, and therefore want no eyes ;
I stumbled when I saw ; full oft 'tis seen,   20
Our means secure us, and our mere defects
Prove our commodities.   Ah, dear son Edgar,
The food of thy abused father's wrath !
Might I but live to see thee in my touch,
I 'ld say I had eyes again !
O.M.   How now, who 's there ?
Edg. (aside) O gods !   Who is 't can say ' I am at the
          worst ' ?
I am worse than e'er I was.
O.M.   'Tis poor mad Tom.
Edg. (aside) And worse I may be yet : the worst is not
As long as we can say ' This is the worst.'
O.M. Fellow, where goest ?
Glo.   Is it a beggar-man ?   30
O.M. Madman, and beggar too.
Glo. 'A has some reason, else he could not beg.
I' the last night's storm I such a fellow saw,
Which made me think a man a worm ; my son
Came then into my mind, and yet my mind
Was then scarce friends with him : I have heard
more since.
As flies are to the wanton boys, are we to the gods ;
They kill us for their sport.
Edg.   (aside) How should this be ?
Bad is the trade that must play the fool to sorrow,
Angering itself and others.   Bless thee, master !   40
Glo. Is that the naked fellow ?
O.M.   Ay, my lord.
Glo. Then, prithee, get thee gone : if for my sake
Thou wilt o'ertake us hence a mile or twain
I' the way toward Dover, do it for ancient love ;
And bring some covering for this naked soul,
Who I 'll entreat to lead me.
O.M.   Alack, sir, he is mad.
Glo. 'Tis the times' plague, when madmen lead the blind.
Do as I bid thee, or rather do thy pleasure ;
Above the rest, be gone.
O.M. I 'll bring him the best 'parel that I have,   50
Come on 't what will.   *Exit*
Glo. Sirrah, naked fellow,—
Edg. Poor Tom 's a-cold.   (aside) I cannot daub it farther.
Glo. Come hither, fellow.
Edg. {(aside) And yet I must.}—Bless thy sweet eyes,
          they bleed.
Glo. Know'st thou the way to Dover ?
Edg. Both stile and gate, horse-way and foot-path.
Poor Tom hath been scar'd out of his good wits.
Bless thee, good man, from the foul fiend !
[Five fiends have been in poor Tom at once ; of   60
lust, as Haberdicat ; Hoberdidance, prince of dumb-
ness ; Maho, of stealing ; Modu, of murder ;
Fliberdigibbet, of mopping and mowing ; who
since possesses chambermaids and waiting-women.
So, bless thee, master !]
Glo. Here, take this purse, thou whom the heavens'
          plagues
Have humbled to all strokes : that I am wretched
Makes thee the happier.   Heavens, deal so still ! ·

Let the superfluous and lust-dicted man,
That stands your ordinance, that will not see   70
Because he does not feel, feel your power quickly ;
So distribution should undo excess
And each man have enough.   Dost thou know Dover ?

Edg. Ay, master.

Glo. There is a cliff whose high and bending head
Looks fearfully in the confined deep :
Bring me but to the very brim of it,
And I'll repair the misery thou dost bear
With something rich about me : from that place
I shall no leading need.

Edg.   Give me thy arm :   80
Poor Tom shall lead thee.   *Exeunt*

SCENE II

Before the Duke of Albany's palace

Enter Goneril and Edmund

Gon. Welcome, my lord : I marvel our mild husband
Not met us on the way.

Enter Oswald

         Now, where 's your master ?

Osw. Madam, within ; but never man so chang'd.
I told him of the army that was landed ;
He smil'd at it : I told him you were coming ;
His answer was, ' The worse :' of Gloucester's
   treachery
And of the loyal service of his son
When I inform'd him, then he call'd me sot,
And told me I had turn'd the wrong side out :
What most he should dislike seems pleasant to him ;   10
What like, offensive.

Gon.   (*to Edm.*) Then shall you go no further.
It is the cowish terror of his spirit,
That dares not undertake : he 'll not feel wrongs,
Which tie him to an answer.   Our wishes on the way
May prove effects.   Back, Edmund, to my brother ;
Hasten his musters, and conduct his powers :
I must change arms at home, and give the distaff
Into my husband's hands.   This trusty servant
Shall pass between us : ere long you are like to hear,
If you dare venture in your own behalf,   20
A mistress's command.   Wear this ; spare speech ;
                Giving a favour
Decline your head ; this kiss, if it durst speak,
Would stretch thy spirits up into the air :
Conceive, and fare thee well.

Edm. Yours in the ranks of death.

Gon.   My most dear Gloucester !
                Exit Edmund
{O, the difference of man and man} !
To thee a woman's services are due :
A fool usurps my bed.

Osw.   Madam, here comes my lord.
                   Exit

Enter Albany

Gon. I have been worth the whistle.

Alb.   O Goneril !
You are not worth the dust which the rude wind   30
Blows in your face.   [I fear your disposition :
That nature which contemns its origin
Cannot be border'd certain in itself ;
She that herself will sliver and disbranch
From her material sap, perforce must wither
And come to deadly use.

Gon. No more, the text is foolish.

Alb. Wisdom and goodness to the vile seem vile,
Filths savour but themselves.   What have you done ?
Tigers, not daughters, what have you perform'd ?   40
A father, and a gracious aged man,
Whose reverence even the head-lugg'd bear would lick,

Most barbarous, most degenerate, have you madded.
Could my good brother suffer you to do it ?
A man, a prince, by him so benefited !
If that the heavens do not their visible spirits
Send quickly down to tame these vile offences,
It will come,
Humanity must perforce prey on itself,
Like monsters of the deep.]

Gon.   Milk-liver'd man !   50
That bear'st a cheek for blows, a head for wrongs ;
Who hast not in thy brows an eye discerning
Thine honour from thy suffering ; [that not know'st,
Fools do those villains pity who are punish'd
Ere they have done their mischief.   Where 's thy
     drum ?
France spreads his banners in our noiseless land,
With plumed helm thy state begins to threat,
Whilst thou, a moral fool, sits still and cries
' Alack, why does he so ?']

Alb.   See thyself, devil !
Proper deformity seems not in the fiend   60
So horrid as in woman.

Gon.   O vain fool !
[*Alb.* Thou changed and self-cover'd thing, for shame,
Be-monster not thy feature.   Were 't my fitness
To let these hands obey my blood,
They are apt enough to dislocate and tear
Thy flesh and bones : howe'er thou art a fiend,
A woman's shape doth shield thee.

Gon. Marry, your manhood mew. . . .

Enter a Messenger

Alb. What news ?]

Mes. O, my good lord, the Duke of Cornwall 's dead,   70
Slain by his servant, going to put out
The other eye of Gloucester.

Alb.   Gloucester's eyes ?

Mes. A servant that he bred, thrill'd with remorse,
Oppos'd against the act, bending his sword
To his great master ; who thereat enrag'd
Flew on him and amongst them fell'd him dead,
But not without that harmful stroke which since
Hath pluck'd him after.

Alb.   This shows you are above,
You justicers, that these our nether crimes
So speedily can venge.   But, O poor Gloucester !   80
Lost he his other eye ?

Mes.   Both, both, my lord.
This letter, madam, craves a speedy answer ;
'Tis from your sister.

Gon.   (*aside*) One way I like this well ;
But being widow, and my Gloucester with her,
May all the building o' my fancy pluck
Upon my hateful life : another way,
The news is not so tart.—I 'll read, and answer.
                   Exit

Alb. Where was his son when they did take his eyes ?

Mes. Come with my lady hither.

Alb.   He is not here.

Mes. No, my good lord ; I met him back again.

Alb. Knows he the wickedness ?   90

Mes. Ay, my good lord ; 'twas he inform'd against him,
And quit the house on purpose, that their punishment
Might have the freer course.

Alb.   Gloucester, I live
To thank thee for the love thou show'dst the king,
And to revenge thine eyes.   Come hither, friend :
Tell me what more thou know'st.   *Exeunt*

[SCENE III

The French camp near Dover

Enter Kent and a Gentleman

Kent. Why the King of France is so suddenly gone back
   know you no reason ?

Gent. Something he left imperfect in the state, which since
   his coming forth is thought of, which imports to the
   kingdom so much fear and danger that his personal
   return was most required and necessary.

Kent. Who hath he left behind him general ?

Gent. The Marshal of France, Monsieur La Far.

Kent. Did your letters pierce the queen to any demon-
   stration of grief ?   10

Gent. I say she took them, read them in my presence,
   And now and then an ample tear trill'd down
   Her delicate cheek : it seem'd she was a queen
   Over her passion, who most rebel-like
   Sought to be king o'er her.

Kent.   O, then it mov'd her.

Gent. Not to a rage ; patience and sorrow strove
   Who should express her goodliest.   You have seen
   Sunshine and rain at once ; her smiles and tears
   Were like, a better way : those happy smilets
   That play'd on her ripe lip seem'd not to know   20
   What guests were in her eyes, which parted thence
   As pearls from diamonds dropp'd ; in brief,
   Sorrow would be a rarity most belov'd,
   If all could so become it.

Kent.   Made she no verbal question ?

Gent. Faith, once or twice she heav'd the name of ' father '
   Pantingly forth, as if it press'd her heart ;
   Cried ' Sisters ! sisters ! Shame of ladies ! sisters !
   Kent ! father ! sisters ! What, i' the storm ! i' the
   night ?
   Let pity not be believed !'   There she shook
   The holy water from her heavenly eyes,   30
   And clamour moisten'd her : then away she started
   To deal with grief alone.

Kent.   It is the stars,
The stars above us, govern our conditions,
Else one self mate and make could not beget
Such different issues.   You spoke not with her since ?

Gent. No.

Kent. Was this before the king return'd ?

Gent.   No, since.

Kent. Well, sir, the poor distressed Lear's i' the town,
Who sometime in his better tune remembers
What we are come about, and by no means   40
Will yield to see his daughter.

Gent.   Why, good sir ?

Kent. A sovereign shame so elbows him, his own un-
   kindness
That stripp'd her from his benediction, turn'd her
To foreign casualties, gave her dear rights
To his dog-hearted daughters, these things sting
His mind so venomously that burning shame
Detains him from Cordelia.

Gent.   Alack, poor gentleman !

Kent. Of Albany's and Cornwall's powers you heard not ?

Gent. 'Tis so they are afoot.

Kent. Well, sir, I 'll bring you to our master Lear,   50
And leave you to attend him : some dear cause
Will in concealment wrap me up awhile ;
When I am known aright, you shall not grieve
Lending me this acquaintance.   I pray you, go
Along with me.   *Exeunt*]

SCENE IV

The same. A tent

*Enter, with drum and colours, Cordelia, Doctor,
and Soldiers*

Cord. Alack, 'tis he : why, he was met even now
    As mad as the vex'd sea, singing aloud,
    Crown'd with rank fumiter and furrow-weeds,
    With hor-docks, hemlock, nettles, cuckoo-flowers,
    Darnel, and all the idle weeds that grow
    In our sustaining corn. A century send forth ;
    Search every acre in the high-grown field,
    And bring him to our eye. [*exit an Officer.*] What
        can man's wisdom
    In the restoring his bereaved sense ?
    He that can help him take all my outward worth.   10
Doc. There is means, madame :
    Our foster-nurse of nature is repose,
    The which he lacks ; that to provoke in him,
    Are many simples operative, whose power
    Will close the eye of anguish.
Cord.   All blest secrets,
    All you unpublish'd virtues of the earth,
    Spring with my tears ! be aidant and remediate
    In the good man's distress ! Seek, seek for him,
    Lest his ungovern'd rage dissolve the life
    That wants the means to lead it.

Enter a Messenger

Mes.   News, madam ;   20
    The British powers are marching hitherward.
Cord. 'Tis known before ; our preparation stands
    In expectation of them. O dear father,
    It is thy business that I go about ;
    Therefore great France
    My mourning and important tears hath pitied.
    No blown ambition doth our arms incite,
    But love, dear love, and our ag'd father's right :
    Soon may I hear and see him !   *Exeunt*

SCENE V

Gloucester's castle

Enter Regan and Oswald

Reg. But are my brother's powers set forth ?
Osw.   Ay, madam.
Reg. Himself in person ?
Osw.   Madam, with much ado :
    Your sister is the better soldier.
Reg. Lord Edmund spake not with your lady at home ?
Osw. No, madam.
Reg. What might import my sister's letters to him ?
Osw. I know not, lady.
Reg. Faith, he is posted hence on serious matter.
    It was great ignorance, Gloucester's eyes being out,
    To let him live : where he arrives he moves   10
    All hearts against us : Edmund, I think, is gone,
    In pity of his misery, to dispatch
    His nighted life ; moreover, to descry
    The strength o' the army.
Osw. I must needs after him, madam, with my letters.
Reg. Our troop sets forth to-morrow, stay with us ;
    The ways are dangerous.
Osw.   I may not, madam,
    My lady charged my duty in this business.
Reg. Why should she write to Edmund ? Might not you
    Transport her purposes by word ? Belike,   20
    Something—I know not what : I 'll love thee much,
    Let me unseal the letter.
Osw.   Madam, I 'd rather—
Reg. I know your lady does not love her husband,
    I am sure of that, and at her late being here
    She gave strange œillades and most speaking looks
    To noble Edmund. I know you are of her bosom.
Osw. Ay, madam.
Reg. I speak in understanding, for I know 't :

    Therefore I do advise you, take this note :
    My lord is dead, Edmund and I have talk'd,   30
    And more convenient is he for my hand
    Than for your lady's ; you may gather more.
    If you do find him, pray you, give him this,
    And when your mistress hears thus much from you,
    I pray, desire her call her wisdom to her.
    So, fare well.
    If you do chance to hear of that blind traitor,
    Preferment falls on him that cuts him off.
Osw. Would I could meet him, madam ! I should show
    What lady I do follow.
Reg.   Fare thee well.   *Exeunt*   40

SCENE VI

Fields near Dover

Enter Gloucester, and Edgar dressed like a peasant

Glo. When shall we come to the top of that same hill ?
Edg. You do climb up it now : look, how we labour.
Glo. Methinks the ground is even.
Edg.   Horrible steep.
    Hark, do you hear the sea ?
Glo.   No, truly.
Edg. Why then your other senses grow imperfect
    By your eyes' anguish.
Glo.   So may it be indeed :
    Methinks thy voice is alter'd, and thou speak'st
    With better phrase and matter than thou didst.
Edg. You 're much deceiv'd : in nothing am I changed
    But in my garments.
Glo.   Methinks you 're better spoken.   10
Edg. Come on, sir, here 's the place, stand still. How
        fearful
    And dizzy 'tis to cast one's eyes so low !
    The crows and choughs that wing the midway air
    Show scarce so gross as beetles ; half way down
    Hangs one that gathers sampire, dreadful trade ;
    Methinks he seems no bigger than his head,
    The fishermen that walk upon the beach
    Appear like mice, and yon tall anchoring bark
    Diminish'd to her cock, her cock, a buoy
    Almost too small for sight : the murmuring surge   20
    That on the unnumber'd idle pebbles chafes
    Cannot be heard : it 's so high, I 'll look no more,
    Lest my brain turn, and the deficient sight
    Topple down headlong.
Glo.   Set me where you stand.
Edg. Give me your hand : you are now within a foot
    Of the extreme verge, for all beneath the moon
    Would I not leap upright.
Glo.   Let go my hand.
    Here, friend, 's another purse, in it a jewel
    Well worth a poor man's taking ; fairies and gods
    Prosper it with thee ! Go thou further off,   30
    Bid me farewell, and let me hear thee going.
Edg. Now fare you well, good sir.
Glo.   With all my heart.
Edg. Why I do trifle thus with his despair
    Is done to cure it.
Glo.   (*kneeling*) O you mighty gods !
    This world I do renounce, and in your sights
    Shake patiently my great affliction off :
    If I could bear it longer and not fall
    To quarrel with your great opposeless wills,
    My snuff and loathed part of nature should
    Burn itself out. If Edgar live, O bless him !   40
    Now, fellow, fare thee well.   *He falls*
Edg.   Gone, sir, farewell.

    And yet I know not how conceit may rob
    The treasury of life, when life itself
    Yields to the theft : had he been where he thought,
    By this had thought been past. Alive or dead ?
    Ho, you sir ! Hear you, sir ! speak !
    Thus might he pass indeed, yet he revives.
    What are you, sir ?
Glo.   Away, and let me die.
Edg. Hadst thou been aught but gossamer, feathers, air,
    So many fathom down precipitating,   50
    Thou hadst shiver'd like an egg, but thou dost
        breathe,
    Hast heavy substance, bleed'st not, speakest, art
        sound.
    Ten masts at each make not the altitude
    Which thou hast perpendicularly fell :
    Thy life 's a miracle. Speak yet again
Glo. But have I fall'n, or no ?
Edg. From the dread summit of this chalky bourn.
    Look up a-height ; the shrill-gorg'd lark so far
    Cannot be seen or heard : do but look up.
Glo. Alack, I have no eyes.   60
    Is wretchedness depriv'd that benefit,
    To end itself by death ? 'Twas yet some comfort,
    When misery could beguile the tyrant's rage
    And frustrate his proud will.
Edg.   Give me your arm :
    Up : so. How feel you your legs ? You stand.
Glo. Too well, too well.
Edg.   This is above all strangeness.
    Upon the crown of the cliff, what thing was that
    Which parted from you ?
Glo.   A poor unfortunate beggar.
Edg. As I stood here below, methought his eyes
    Were two full moons ; 'a had a thousand noses,   70
    Horns, whelk'd and waved like the enridged sea :
    It was some fiend ; therefore, thou happy father,
    Think that the clearest gods, who made their honours
    Of men's impossibilities, have preserv'd thee.
Glo. I do remember now : henceforth I 'll bear
    Affliction till it do cry out itself
    'Enough, enough,' and die. That thing you speak of
    I took it for a man ; often would it say
    ' The fiend, the fiend :' he led me to that place.
Edg. Bear free and patient thoughts. But who comes here ?   80
    Enter Lear, fantastically dressed with wild flowers
    The safer sense will ne'er accommodate
    His master thus.
Lear. No, they cannot touch me for coining ; I am the
    king himself.
Edg. O thou side-piercing sight !
Lear. Nature is above art in that respect. There 's your
    press-money. That fellow handles his bow like a
    crow-keeper ; draw me a clothier's yard. Look,
    look, a mouse ! Peace, peace ; this toasted cheese
    will do it. There 's my gauntlet ; I 'll prove it on a   90
    giant. Bring up the brown bills. O, well flown,
    bird in the air ! hagh ! Give the word.
Edg. Sweet marjoram.
Lear. Pass.
Glo. I know that voice.
Lear. Ha, Goneril, ha, Regan ! They flattered me like a
    dog, and told me I had white hairs in my beard ere
    the black ones were there. To say 'ay' and 'no'
    to every thing I said 'ay' and 'no' to was no good
    divinity. When the rain came to wet me once, and   100
    the wind to make me chatter, when the thunder
    would not peace at my bidding, there I found them,
    there I smelt them out. Go to, they are not men of
    their words : they told me I was every thing ; 'tis a
    lie, I am not ague-proof.

CARL A. RUDISILL LIBRARY
LENOIR RHYNE COLLEGE

Glo. The trick of that voice I do well remember :
　Is 't not the king ?

Lear.　　　　　　Ay, every inch a king :
　When I do stare, see how the subject quakes.
　I pardon that man's life.　What was thy cause ?
　Adultery ?　　　　　　　　　　　　　　　110
　Thou shalt not die for adultery, no :
　The wren goes to 't, and the small gilded fly
　Does lecher in my sight.
　Let copulation thrive, for Gloucester's bastard son
　Was kinder to his father than my daughters
　Got 'tween the lawful sheets.
　To 't luxury, pell-mell, for I lack soldiers.
　Behold yon simpering dame,
　Whose face between her forks presageth snow,
　That minces virtue, and does shake the head　120
　To hear of pleasure's name ;
　The fitchew nor the soiled horse goes to 't
　With a more riotous appetite.
　Down from the waist they 're Centaurs,
　Though women all above :
　But to the girdle do the gods inherit,
　Beneath is all the fiends' ;
　There 's hell, there 's darkness, there 's the sulphury pit,
　Burning, scalding, stench, consumption ; fie, fie,
　fie ! pah, pah ! Give me an ounce of civet, good　130
　apothecary, to sweeten my imagination : there 's
　money for thee.

Glo. O, let me kiss that hand !

Lear. Here, wipe it first, it smells of mortality.

Glo. O ruin'd piece of nature !　This great world
　Should so wear out to nought.　Do you know me ?

Lear. I remember thy eyes well enough.　Dost thou
　squiny on me ? No, do thy worst, blind Cupid ;
　I 'll not love.　Read thou that challenge, mark
　the penning of 't.　　　　　　　　　　　140

Glo. Were all the letters suns, I could not see one.

Edg. I would not take this from report : it is,
　And my heart breaks at it.

Lear. Read.

Glo. What, with the case of eyes ?

Lear. O, ho, are you there with me ? No eyes in your
　head, nor no money in your purse ? Your eyes are
　in a heavy case, your purse in a light, yet you see
　how this world goes.

Glo. I see it feelingly.　　　　　　　　　150

Lear. What, art mad ?　A man may see how the world
　goes with no eyes.　Look with thy ears : see
　how yon justice rails upon yon simple thief.　Hark
　in thy ear : handy-dandy, which is the thief, which
　is the justice ?　Thou hast seen a farmer's dog
　bark at a beggar ?

Glo. Ay, sir.

Lear. And the creature run from the cur ?　There thou
　mightst behold the great image of authority : a
　dog 's obey'd in office.
　Thou rascal beadle, hold thy bloody hand !　161
　Why dost thou lash that whore ?　Strip thine own
　　back ;
　Thy blood hotly lusts to use her in that kind
　For which thou whip'st her ; the usurer hangs the
　　cozener.
　Through tatter'd rags small vices do appear,
　Robes and furr'd gowns hides all.　{Plate sins with gold,
　And the strong lance of justice hurtless breaks ;
　Arm it in rags, a pigmy's straw does pierce it.
　None does offend, none, I say, none ; I 'll able 'em :
　Take that of me, my friend, who have the power　170
　To seal the accuser's lips.}　Get thee glass eyes,
　And, like a scurvy politician, seem
　To see the things thou dost not.

No now, pull off my boots : harder, harder : so.

Edg. O, matter and impertinency mix'd !
　Reason in madness !

Lear. If thou wilt weep my fortune, take my eyes.
　I know thee well enough, thy name is Gloucester,
　Thou must be patient ; we came crying hither :
　Thou knowest, the first time that we smell the air,　180
　We wail and cry.　I will preach to thee, mark me.

Glo. Alack, alack the day !

Lear. When we are born, we cry that we are come
　To this great stage of fools, this a good block.
　It were a delicate stratagem, to shoe
　A troop of horse with felt : {I 'll put 't in proof ;}
　And when I have stol'n upon these son-in-laws,
　Then kill, kill, kill, kill, kill, kill !

Enter three Gentlemen

Gent. O, here he is ; lay hands upon him, sirs,
　Your most dear—　　　　　　　　　　190

Lear. No rescue ?　What, a prisoner ?　I am even
　The natural fool of fortune.　Use me well,
　You shall have ransom.　Let me have a surgeon ;
　I am cut to the brains.

Gent.　　　　　　You shall have any thing.

Lear. No seconds ?　all myself ?
　Why, this would make a man of salt,
　To use his eyes for garden water-pots,
　[Aye, and laying autumn's dust.]

Gent. Good sir,—

Lear. I will die bravely, like a bridegroom.　What ?　200
　I will be jovial : come, come ; I am a king,
　My masters, know you that.

Gent. You are a royal one, and we obey you.

Lear. Then there 's life in 't.　Nay, an you get it, you
　　shall get it with running.

Exit running ; Attendants follow.

Gent. A sight most pitiful in the meanest wretch,
　Past speaking of in a king !　Thou hast one daughter,
　Who redeems nature from the general curse
　Which twain have brought her to.

Edg. Hail, gentle sir.

Gent.　　　　　Sir, speed you, what 's your will ?　210

Edg. Do you hear aught of a battle toward ?

Gent. Most sure and vulgar : every one hears that,
　Which can distinguish sense.

Edg.　　　　　But, by your favour,
　How near 's the other army ?

Gent. Near, and on speedy foot ; the main descry
　Stands on the hourly thought.

Edg.　　　　　I thank you, sir : that 's all.

Gent. Though that the queen on special cause is here,
　Her army is mov'd on.

Edg.　　　　　I thank you, sir.　*Exit Gent.*

Glo. You ever-gentle gods, take my breath from me ;
　Let not my worser spirit tempt me again　　　220
　To die before you please !

Edg.　　　　　Well, pray you, father.

Glo. Now, good sir, what are you ?

Edg. A most poor man, made lame by fortune's blows,
　Who, by the art of known and feeling sorrows,
　Am pregnant to good pity.　Give me your hand,
　I 'll lead you to some biding.

Glo.　　　　　Hearty thanks ;
　The bounty and the benison of heaven
　To save thee !

Enter Oswald

Osw.　　　　A proclaim'd prize !　Most happy !
　That eyeless head of thine was framed flesh
　To raise my fortunes.　Thou most unhappy traitor,　230
　Briefly thyself remember, the sword is out
　That must destroy thee.

Glo.　　　　Now let thy friendly hand
　Put strength enough to 't.　*Edgar interposes*

Osw.　　　　Wherefore, bold peasant,
　Durst thou support a publish'd traitor ?　Hence,
　Lest the infection of his fortune take
　Like hold on thee.　Let go his arm.

Edg. Chill not let go, sir, without 'cagion.

Osw. Let go, slave, or thou diest !

Edg. Good gentleman, go your gait, let poor volk pass.
　An chud have been swagger'd out of my life, it　240
　would not have been so long by a vortnight.　Nay,
　come not near the old man ; keep out, che vor ye, or
　I 'll try whether your costard or my ballow be the
　harder : I 'll be plain with you.

Osw. Out, dunghill !　　　　　　　*They fight*

Edg. Chill pick your teeth, sir : come ; no matter for
　your foins.

Oswald falls

Osw. Slave, thou hast slain me.　Villain, take my purse :
　If ever thou wilt thrive, bury my body,
　And give the letters which thou find'st about me　250
　To Edmund Earl of Gloucester ; seek him out
　Upon the British party.　O, untimely death !
　Death !　　　　　　　　　　　　　*Dies*

Edg. I know thee well, a serviceable villain,
　As duteous to the vices of thy mistress
　As badness would desire.

Glo.　　　　　What, is he dead ?

Edg. Sit you down, father ; rest you.
　Let 's see his pockets : these letters that he speaks of
　May be my friends.　He 's dead ; I am only sorry
　He had no other deathsman.　Let us see :　　260
　Leave, gentle wax ; and, manners, blame us not :
　To know our enemies' minds, we 'ld rip their hearts ;
　Their papers, is more lawful.
　(*reads*) ' Let your reciprocal vows be remembered.
　You have many opportunities to cut him off : if your
　will want not, time and place will be fruitfully
　offered.　There is nothing done, if he return the
　conqueror, then am I the prisoner, and his bed my
　gaol, from the loathed warmth whereof deliver
　me, and supply the place for your labour.　　270
　　Your wife (so I would say)
　　　　　　your affectionate servant,
　　[and for you her own for venter,]
　　　　　　　　' GONERIL.'
　O undistinguish'd space of woman's wit !
　A plot upon her virtuous husband's life,
　And the exchange my brother !　Here, in the sands,
　Thee I 'll rake up, the post unsanctified
　Of murderous lechers, and in the mature time
　With this ungracious paper strike the sight　　280
　Of the death-practis'd duke : for him 'tis well
　That of thy death and business I can tell.

Glo. The king is mad : how stiff is my vile sense,
　That I stand up, and have ingenious feeling
　Of my huge sorrows !　Better I were distract :
　So should my thoughts be fenced from my griefs,
　And woes by wrong imaginations lose
　The knowledge of themselves.　*Drum afar off*

Edg.　　　　Give me your hand :
　Far off, methinks, I hear the beaten drum :
　Come, father, I'll bestow you with a friend.　290

Exeunt

SCENE VII

*A tent in the French camp.　Lear on a bed asleep, soft
music playing ; Gentleman, and others standing*

Enter Cordelia, Kent, and Doctor

Cord. O thou good Kent, how shall I live and work,
    To match thy goodness? My life will be too short,
    And every measure fail me.
Kent. To be acknowledg'd, madam, is o'erpaid.
    All my reports go with the modest truth,
    Nor more, nor clipp'd, but so.
Cord.   Be better suited:
    These weeds are memories of those worser hours,
    I prithee, put them off.
Kent.   Pardon me, dear madam;
    Yet to be known shortens my made intent:
    My boon I make it, that you know me not   10
    Till time and I think meet.
Cord. Then be 't so, my good lord. (*to the Doctor*) How
    does the king?
Doc. Madame, sleeps still.
Cord. O you kind gods,
    Cure this great breach in his abused nature!
    The untun'd and hurrying senses, O, wind up
    Of this child-changed father!
Doc.   So please your majesty
    That we may wake the king; he hath slept long.
Cord. Be govern'd by your knowledge, and proceed   20
    I' the sway of your own will. Is he array'd?
Gent. Ay, madam, in the heaviness of his sleep
    We put fresh garments on him.
Doc. Good madam, be by when we do awake him;
    I doubt not of his temperance.
[*Cord.*   Very well.
Doc. Please you, draw near. Louder the music there I]
Cord. O my dear father! Restoration hang
    Thy medicine on my lips, and let this kiss
    Repair those violent harms that my two sisters
    Have in thy reverence made!
Kent.   Kind and dear princess!   30
Cord. Had you not been their father, these white flakes
    Had challenged pity of them. Was this a face
    To be expos'd against the warring winds?
    [To stand against the deep dread-bolted thunder?
    In the most terrible and nimble stroke
    Of quick cross lightning? to watch—poor perdu!—
    With this thin helm?] Mine injurer's dog,
    Though he had bit me, should have stood that night
    Against my fire, and wast thou fain, poor father,
    To hovel thee with swine and rogues forlorn,   40
    In short and musty straw? Alack, alack!
    'Tis wonder that thy life and wits at once
    Had not concluded all. He wakes; speak to him.
Doc. Madam, do you; 'tis fittest.
Cord. How does my royal lord? How fares your majesty?
Lear. You do me wrong to take me out o' the grave:
    Thou art a soul in bliss, but I am bound
    Upon a wheel of fire, that mine own tears
    Do scald like molten lead.
Cord.   Sir, know me.
Lear. You are a spirit, I know, where did you die?   50
Cord. Still, still, far wide!
Doc. He 's scarce awake, let him alone awhile.
Lear. Where have I been? Where am I? Fair daylight?
    I am mightily abus'd. I should e'en die with pity,
    To see another thus. I know not what to say.
    I will not swear these are my hands: let 's see;
    I feel this pin prick. Would I were assur'd
    Of my condition!
Cord.   O, look upon me, sir,
    And hold your hands in benediction o'er me.
    No, sir, you must not kneel.
Lear.   Pray, do not mock: 60
    I am a very foolish fond old man,
    Fourscore and upward, {not an hour more nor less;}
    And, to deal plainly,

I fear I am not in my perfect mind.
Methinks I should know you, and know this man;
Yet I am doubtful, for I am mainly ignorant
What place this is, and all the skill I have
Remembers not these garments, nor I know not
Where I did lodge last night. Do not laugh at me,
For, as I am a man, I think this lady   70
To be my child Cordelia.
Cord.   And so I am.
Lear. Be your tears wet? yes, faith. I pray, weep not:
    If you have poison for me, I will drink it.
    I know you do not love me, for your sisters
    Have, as I do remember, done me wrong:
    You have some cause, they have not.
Cord.   No cause, no cause.
Lear. Am I in France?
Kent.   In your own kingdom, sir.
Lear. Do not abuse me.
Doc. Be comforted, good madame: the great rage,
    You see, is cur'd in him: [and yet it is danger   80
    To make him even o'er the time he has lost.]
    Desire him to go in, trouble him no more
    Till further settling.
Cord. Will 't please your highness walk?
Lear.   You must bear with me.
    Pray now, forget and forgive: I am old and foolish.
           Exeunt all but Kent and Gentleman
[*Gent.* Holds it true, sir, that the Duke of Cornwall was
    so slain?
Kent. Most certain, sir.
Gent. Who is conductor of his people?
Kent. As 'tis said, the bastard son of Gloucester.   90
Gent. They say Edgar, his banished son, is with the Earl
    of Kent in Germany.
Kent. Report is changeable. 'Tis time to look about,
    the powers of the kingdom approach apace.
Gent. The arbitrement is like to be bloody. Fare you
    well, sir.   *Exit*
Kent. My point and period will be throughly wrought,
    Or well or ill, as this day's battle 's fought.   *Exit*

Act Fifth

SCENE I

The British camp near Dover

*Enter, with drum and colours, Edmund, Regan,
Gentleman, and Soldiers*

Edm. Know of the duke if his last purpose hold,
    Or whether since he is advis'd by aught
    To change the course: he 's full of abdication
    And self-reproving; bring his constant pleasure.
           To a Gentleman, who goes out
Reg. Our sister's man is certainly miscarried.
Edm. 'Tis to be doubted, madam.
Reg.   Now, sweet lord,
    You know the goodness I intend upon you,
    Tell me but truly, but then speak the truth,
    Do you not love my sister?
Edm.   Ay, honour'd love.
Reg. But have you never found my brother's way,   10
    To the forfended place?
[*Edm.*   That thought abuses you.
Reg. I am doubtful that you have been conjunct

    And bosom'd with her, as far as we call hers.]
Edm. No, by mine honour, madam.

Reg. I never shall endure her; dear my lord,
    Be not familiar with her.
Edm.   Fear me not.—
    She and the duke her husband!

      *Enter, with drum and colours, Albany, Goneril,
      and Soldiers*

[*Gon.* (*aside*) I had rather lose the battle than that sister
    Should loosen him and me.]
Alb. Our very loving sister, well be-met.   20
    For this I hear; the king is come to his daughter,
    With others, whom the rigour of our state
    Forc'd to cry out. [Where I could not be honest,
    I never yet was valiant: for this business,
    It toucheth us, as France invades our land,
    Not bolds the king, with others, whom, I fear,
    Most just and heavy causes make oppose.
Edm. Sir, you speak nobly.
Reg.   Why is this reason'd?
Gon. Combine together 'gainst the enemy;
    For these domestic dear particulars
    Are not to question here.
Alb.   Let us then determine   31
    With the ancient of war on our proceedings.
[*Edm.* I shall attend you presently at your tent.]
Reg. Sister, you 'll go with us?
Gon. No.
Reg. 'Tis most convenient; pray you, go with us.
Gon. (*aside*) O, ho, I know the riddle.—I will go.

    As they are going out, enter Edgar disguised
Edg. If e'er your grace had speech with man so poor,
    Hear me one word.
Alb.   I 'll overtake you. Speak.
        Exeunt all but Albany and Edgar

Edg. Before you fight the battle, ope this letter.   40
    If you have victory, let the trumpet sound
    For him that brought it: wretched though I seem,
    I can produce a champion that will prove
    What is avouched there. If you miscarry,
    Your business of the world hath so an end,
    {And machination ceases.} Fortune love you!
Alb. Stay till I have read the letter.
Edg.   I was forbid it.
    When time shall serve, let but the herald cry,
    And I 'll appear again.
Alb. Why, fare thee well: I will o'erlook the paper.   50
          Exit Edgar

      Re-enter Edmund
Edm. The enemy 's in view, draw up your powers.
    Hard is the guess of their great strength and forces
    By diligent discovery; but your haste
    Is now urg'd on you.
Alb.   We will greet the time.   *Exit*

Edm. To both these sisters have I sworn my love;
    Each jealous of the other, as the stung
    Are of the adder. Which of them shall I take?
    Both, one, or neither? Neither can be enjoy'd,
    If both remain alive: to take the widow
    Exasperates, makes mad her sister Goneril;   60
    And hardly shall I carry out my side,
    Her husband being alive. Now then we 'll use
    His countenance for the battle, which being done,
    Let her that would be rid of him devise
    His speedy taking off. As for his mercy
    Which he intends to Lear and to Cordelia,
    The battle done, and they within our power,
    Shall never see his pardon; for my state
    Stands on me to defend, not to debate.   *Exit*

SCENES II AND III

A field between the two camps

*Enter the powers of France over the stage, Cordelia
with her father in her hand ; and exeunt*

Enter Edgar and Gloucester

Edg. Here, father, take the shadow of this bush
For your good host ; pray that the right may thrive :
If ever I return to you again,
I 'll bring you comfort.

Glo.   Grace go with you, sir !

                                                   Exit Edgar

Alarum and retreat within.   Re-enter Edgar

Edg. Away, old man ; give me thy hand ; away !
King Lear hath lost, he and his daughter ta'en :
Give me thy hand ; come on.

Glo. No farther, sir ; a man may rot even here.

Edg. What, in ill thoughts again ?   Men must endure
Their going hence, even as their coming hither :   10
Ripeness is all : come on.

Glo.   {And that 's true too.}

                                                  Exeunt

*Enter, in conquest, with drum and colours, Edmund ; Lear
and Cordelia, as prisoners ; Captain, Soldiers, etc.*

Edm. Some officers take them away : good guard,
Until their greater pleasures best be known
That are to censure them.

Cord.   We are not the first
Who with best meaning have incurr'd the worst.
For thee, oppressed king, am I cast down ;
Myself could else out-frown false fortune's frown.
Shall we not see these daughters, and these sisters ?

Lear. No, no !   Come, let 's away to prison :
We two alone will sing like birds i' the cage :
When thou dost ask me blessing, I 'll kneel down   10
And ask of thee forgiveness : so we 'll live,
And pray, and sing, and tell old tales, and laugh
At gilded butterflies, and hear poor rogues
Talk of court news ; and we 'll talk with them too,
Who loses and who wins, who 's in, who 's out,
And take upon 's the mystery of things,
As if we were God's spies ; and we 'll wear out,
In a wall'd prison, packs and sects of great ones
That ebb and flow by the moon.

Edm.   Take them away.

Lear. Upon such sacrifices, my Cordelia,   20
The gods themselves throw incense ; have I caught
     thee ?
He that parts us shall bring a brand from heaven,
And fire us hence like foxes.   Wipe thine eyes ;
The good years shall devour them, flesh and fell,
Ere they shall make us weep : we 'll see 'em starve
     first.
Come.   *Exeunt Lear and Cordelia, guarded*

Edm. Come hither, captain ; hark.
Take thou this note, go follow them to prison :
One step I have advanc'd thee ; if thou dost
As this instructs thee, thou dost make thy way
To noble fortunes : know thou this, that men
Are as the time is : to be tender-minded   30
Does not become a sword : thy great employment
Will not bear question ; either say thou 'lt do 't,
Or thrive by other means.

Cap.   I 'll do 't, my lord.

Edm. About it, and write happy when thou hast done.
Mark, I say instantly, and carry it so
As I have set it down.

{*Cap.* I cannot draw a cart, nor eat dried oats ;
If it be man's work, I 'll do 't.   *Exit*]

*Flourish.   Enter Albany, Goneril, Regan, another Captain,
and Soldiers*

Alb. Sir, you have show'd to-day your valiant strain,   40
And fortune led you well : you have the captives
That were the opposites of this day's strife :
We do require them of you, so to use them
As we shall find their merits and our safety
May equally determine.

Edm.   Sir, I thought it fit
To send the old and miserable king
To some retention and appointed guard ;
Whose age has charms in it, whose title more,
To pluck the common bosom of his side,
And turn our impress'd lances in our eyes   50
Which do command them.   With him I sent the
     queen :
My reason all the same ; and they are ready
To-morrow or at further space to appear
Where you shall hold your session.   [At this time
We sweat and bleed : the friend hath lost his friend ;
And the best quarrels, in the heat, are curs'd
By those that feel their sharps.
The question of Cordelia and her father
Requires a fitter place.]

Alb.   Sir, by your patience,
I hold you but a subject of this war,   60
Not as a brother.

Reg.   That 's as we list to grace him.
Methinks our pleasure might have been demanded,
Ere you had spoke so far.   He led our powers,
Bore the commission of my place and person ;
The which immediacy may well stand up
And call itself your brother.

Gon.   Not so hot :
In his own grace he doth exalt himself
More than in your advancement.

Reg.   In my right,
By me invested, he compeers the best.

Gon. That were the most, if he should husband you.   70

Reg. Jesters do oft prove prophets.

Gon.   Hola, hola !
That eye that told you so look'd but a-squint.

Reg. Lady, I am not well, else I should answer
From a full-flowing stomach.   General,
Take thou my soldiers, prisoners, patrimony ;
{Dispose of them, of me ; the walls is thine :}
Witness the world, that I create thee here
My lord and master.

Gon.   Mean you to enjoy him then ?

Alb. The let alone lies not in your good will.

Edm. Nor in thine, lord.

Alb.   Half-blooded fellow, yes.   80

Edm. Let the drum strike, and prove my title good.

Alb. Stay yet, hear reason.   Edmund, I arrest thee
On capital treason, and in thine attaint
This gilded serpent (*pointing to Gon.*).   For your claim,
     fair sister,
I bar it in the interest of my wife ;
'Tis she is sub-contracted to this lord,
And I, her husband, contradict your banns.
If you will marry, make your loves to me ;
My lady is bespoke.

{*Gon.*   An interlude !}

Alb. Thou art arm'd, Gloucester : {let the trumpet sound :}
If none appear to prove upon thy head   91
Thy heinous, manifest, and many treasons,
There is my pledge (*throwing down a glove*) : I 'll prove
     it on thy heart,
Ere I taste bread, thou art in nothing less
Than I have here proclaim'd thee.

Reg.   Sick, O, sick !

Gon. (*aside*) If not, I 'll ne'er trust poison.

Edm. (*throwing down a glove*) There 's my exchange : what
in the world he is
That names me traitor, villain-like he lies :
Call by thy trumpet : he that dares approach,
On him, on you,—who not ?—I will maintain   100
My truth and honour firmly.

Alb. A herald, ho !

Edm.   A herald, ho, a herald !

Alb. Trust to thy single virtue, for thy soldiers,
All levied in my name, have in my name
Took their discharge.

Reg.   This sickness grows upon me.

Alb. She is not well ; convey her to my tent.

                         Enter a Herald   *Exit Regan, led*

Come hither, herald,—Let the trumpet sound,—
And read out this.

Cap. Sound, trumpet !   *A trumpet sounds*

Her. (*reads*) 'If any man of quality or degree within   110
the host of the army will maintain upon Edmund,
suppos'd Earl of Gloucester, that he 's a manifold
traitor, let him appear at the third sound of the
trumpet : he is bold in his defence.'

Edm. Sound !   Again !

     Enter Edgar, at the third sound, a trumpet before him

Alb. Ask him his purposes, why he appears
Upon this call o' the trumpet.

Her.   What are you ?
Your name and quality ? and why you answer
This present summons ?

Edg.   O know, my name is lost
By treason's tooth ; bare-gnawn and canker-bit :   120
Yet am I noble.   Where is the adversary
I come to cope withal ?

Alb.   Which is that adversary ?

Edg. What 's he that speaks for Edmund, Earl of Gloucester ?

Edm. Himself : what say'st thou to him ?

Edg.   Draw thy sword,
That if my speech offend a noble heart,
Thy arm may do thee justice : here is mine.
Behold, it is the privilege of my tongue,
My oath, and my profession : I protest,
Maugre thy strength, youth, place and eminence,
Despite thy victor sword and fire-new fortune,   130
Thy valour and thy heart, thou art a traitor,
False to thy gods, thy brother and thy father,
Conspirant 'gainst this high illustrious prince,
And from the extremest upward of thy head
To the descent and dust beneath thy feet,
A most toad-spotted traitor.   Say thou 'No,'
This sword, this arm and my best spirits are bent
To prove upon thy heart, whereto I speak,
Thou liest.

Edm.   In wisdom I should ask thy name,   140
But since thy outside looks so fair and warlike
And that thy tongue some say of breeding breathes,
{What safe and nicely I might well delay}
By right of knighthood, I disdain and spurn :
Here do I toss those treasons to thy head ;
With the hell-hated lie o'erwhelm thy heart ;
Which for they yet glance by and scarcely bruise,
This sword of mine shall give them instant way,
Where they shall rest for ever.   Trumpets, speak !

                    Alarums.   They fight.   Edmund falls

Alb. Save him, save him !

Gon.   This is mere practice, Gloucester :   150
By the law of arms thou art not bound to answer
An unknown opposite ; thou art not vanquish'd,
But cozen'd and beguil'd.

Alb.   Stop your mouth, dame,
Or with this paper shall I stopple it.
Thou worse than any thing, read thine own evil.
Nay, no tearing, lady, I perceive you know it.

Gon. Say, if I do, the laws are mine, not thine :
    Who shall arraign me for 't ?
Alb.   Most monstrous !
    Know'st thou this paper ?
Gon.   Ask me not what I know.
                                                                Exit
Alb. Go after her, she 's desperate, govern her.   160
Edm. What you have charg'd me with, that have I done,
    And more, much more, the time will bring it out :
    'Tis past, and so am I ; but what art thou
    That hast this fortune on me ? If thou be'st noble,
    I do forgive thee.
Edg.   Let 's exchange charity.
    I am no less in blood than thou art, Edmund ;
    If more, the more thou hast wrong'd me.
    My name is Edgar, and thy father's son.
    The gods are just, and of our pleasant vices
    Make instruments to scourge us :   170
    The dark and vicious place where thee he got
    Cost him his eyes.
Edm.   Thou hast spoken truth ;
    The wheel is come full circle ; I am here.
Alb. Methought thy very gait did prophesy
    A royal nobleness : I must embrace thee :
    Let sorrow split my heart, if I did ever
    Hate thee or thy father !
Edg.   Worthy prince, I know 't.
Alb. Where have you hid yourself ?
    How have you known the miseries of your father ?
Edg. By nursing them, my lord.   List a brief tale,   180
    And when 'tis told, O, that my heart would burst !
    The bloody proclamation to escape
    That follow'd me so near,—O, our lives' sweetness :
    That with the pain of death would hourly die
    Rather than die at once !—taught me to shift
    Into a madman's rags, to assume a semblance
    That very dogs disdain'd : and in this habit
    Met I my father with his bleeding rings,
    Their precious stones new lost ; became his guide,
    Led him, begg'd for him, saved him from despair ;   190
    Never—O Father !—reveal'd myself unto him,
    Until some half-hour past, when I was arm'd,
    Not sure, though hoping of this good success,
    I ask'd his blessing, and from first to last
    Told him my pilgrimage, but his flaw'd heart,
    Alack, too weak the conflict to support,
    'Twixt two extremes of passion, joy and grief,
    Burst smilingly.
Edm.   This speech of yours hath mov'd me,
    And shall perchance do good ; but speak you on,
    You look as you had something more to say.   200
Alb. If there be more, more woful, hold it in,
    For I am almost ready to dissolve,
    Hearing of this.
[*Edg.*   This would have seem'd a period
    To such as love not sorrow ; but another,
    To amplify too much, would make much more.
    And top extremity.   Whilst I
    Was big in clamour, came there in a man,
    Who, having seen me in my worst estate,
    Shunn'd my abhorr'd society, but then, finding
    Who 'twas that so endur'd, with his strong arms   210
    He fasten'd on my neck, and bellow'd out
    As he 'ld burst heaven, threw me on my father,
    Told the most piteous tale of Lear and him
    That ever ear receiv'd : which in recounting
    His grief grew puissant, and the strings of life
    Began to crack : twice then the trumpet sounded,
    And there I left him tranc'd.
Alb.   But who was this ?
Edg. Kent, sir, the banish'd Kent, who in disguise
    Follow'd his enemy king, and did him service

    Improper for a slave.]   220
                            Enter one with a bloody knife
Gent. Help, help !
Alb.   What kind of help ?
    What means that bloody knife ?
Gent.   It 's hot, it smokes ;
    It came even from the heart of—
Alb. Who, man ? Speak !
Gent. Your lady, sir, your lady : and her sister
    By her is poisoned ; she hath confess'd it.
Edm. I was contracted to them both : all three
    Now marry in an instant.
Alb. Produce the bodies, be they alive or dead.
                                        Exit Gentleman
    This justice of the heavens, that makes us tremble,   230
    Touches us not with pity.
Edg.   Here comes Kent, sir.
                            Enter Kent
Alb.   O, 'tis he ;
    The time will not allow the compliment
    That very manners urges.
Kent.   I am come
    To bid my king and master aye good night :
    Is he not here ?
Alb.   Great thing of us forgot !
    Speak, Edmund, where 's the king ? and where 's
        Cordelia ?
    See'st thou this object, Kent ?
                The bodies of Goneril and Regan are brought in
Kent. Alack, why thus ?
Edm.   Yet Edmund was belov'd :
    The one the other poison'd for my sake,
    And after slew herself.   240
Alb. Even so.   Cover their faces.
Edm. I pant for life : some good I mean to do,
    Despite of mine own nature.   Quickly send,
    Be brief in 't, to the castle, for my writ
    Is on the life of Lear and on Cordelia :
    Nay, send in time.
Alb.   Run, run, O, run !
Edg. To who, my lord ?   Who hath the office ? send
    Thy token of reprieve.
Edm. Well thought on, take my sword, the captain,
    Give it the captain.
Alb.   Haste thee, for thy life.   250
                                        Exit Edgar
Edm. He hath commission from thy wife and me
    To hang Cordelia in the prison, and
    To lay the blame upon her own despair,
    That she fordid herself.
Alb. The gods defend her !   Bear him hence awhile.
                                        Edmund is borne off
    Enter Lear, with Cordelia in his arms ; Edgar, Captain,
                        and others following
Lear. Howl, howl, howl, howl !   O, you are men of stones :
    Had I your tongues and eyes, I would use them so
    That heaven's vault should crack.   She 's gone for
        ever !
    I know when one is dead and when one lives ;
    She 's dead as earth.   Lend me a looking-glass,   260
    If that her breath will mist or stain the stone,
    Why then she lives.
Kent.   Is this the promis'd end ?
Edg. Or image of that horror ?
Alb.   Fall and cease.
Lear. This feather stirs, she lives ; if it be so,
    It is a chance which does redeem all sorrows
    That ever I have felt.
Kent.   Ah my good master !
Lear. Prithee, away.
Edg.   'Tis noble Kent, your friend.

Lear. A plague upon you murderous traitors all !
    I might have sav'd her ; now she 's gone for ever !
    Cordelia, Cordelia, stay a little.   Ha !   270
    What is 't thou say'st ?   Her voice was ever soft,
    Gentle and low, an excellent thing in women.
    I kill'd the slave that was a-hanging thee.
Capt. 'Tis true, my lords, he did.
Lear.   Did I not, fellow ?
    I have seen the day, with my good biting falchion
    I would have made them skip : I am old now,
    And these same crosses spoil me.   Who are you ?
    Mine eyes are not o' the best, I 'll tell you straight.
Kent. If fortune bragg'd of two she lov'd or hated,
    One of them we behold.   280
Lear. {This is a dull sight.}   Are not you Kent ?
Kent.   The same,
    Your servant Kent.   Where is your servant Caius ?
Lear. He 's a good fellow, I can tell that ;
    He 'll strike, and quickly too : he 's dead and rotten.
Kent. No, my good lord ; I am the very man—
Lear. I 'll see that straight.
Kent. That from your first of difference and decay
    Have follow'd your sad steps.
Lear.   You 're welcome hither.
Kent. Nor no man else : all 's cheerless, dark and deadly.
    Your eldest daughters have fordone themselves,   290
    And desperately are dead.
Lear.   So think I too.
Alb. He knows not what he sees, and vain is it
    That we present us to him.
Edg.   Very bootless.
                    Enter a Captain
Capt. Edmund is dead, my lord.
Alb.   That 's but a trifle here.
    You lords and noble friends, know our intent.
    What comfort to this decay may come
    Shall be applied : for us, we will resign,
    During the life of this old majesty,
    To him our absolute power : (*to Edgar and Kent*) you,
        to your rights ;
    With boot, and such addition as your honours   300
    Have more than merited.   All friends shall taste
    The wages of their virtue, and all foes
    The cup of their deservings.   O, see, see !
Lear. And my poor fool is hang'd !   No, no life !
    Why should a dog, a horse, a rat, have life,
    And thou no breath at all ?   O thou wilt come
    No more ; never, never, never. {never ; never.}
    Pray you, undo this button : thank you, sir.
    [Oh, oh, oh, oh !]   {Do you see this !   Look on
        her, look, her lips,
    Look there, look there !}
Edg.   He faints.   My lord, my lord !   310
Lear. Break, heart ; I prithee, break !
Edg.   Look up, my lord.
Kent. Vex not his ghost : O, let him pass ! he hates him
    That would upon the rack of this tough world
    Stretch him out longer.   *Lear dies*
Edg.   O, he is gone indeed.
Kent. The wonder is he hath endur'd so long :
    He but usurp'd his life.
Alb. Bear them from hence.   Our present business
    Is to general woe. (*to Kent and Edgar*) Friends of
        my soul, you twain
    Rule in this kingdom and the gor'd state sustain.
Kent. I have a journey, sir, shortly to go ;   320
    My master calls, and I must not say no.
Alb. The weight of this sad time we must obey,
    Speak what we feel, not what we ought to say.
    The oldest have borne most : we that are young
    Shall never see so much, nor live so long.
                            Exeunt, with a dead march

Notes

I. i. 76. *precious square of sense*; this is a characteristically compressed phrase, which must, I think, mean 'the senses when applying their most exacting standard.'

I. i. 85. F reads

> *Although our last and least; to whose young love,*
> *The Vines of France, and Milke of Burgundie,*
> *Strive to be interest.*

I. i. 96-105. *Cf.* Desdemona to Brabantio, *Othello*, I. iii.

I. i. 111. *mysteries*; Q, *mistresse*; F, *miseries.*

I. i. 174. *Our potency made good*; obscure; perhaps simply 'if my power is to maintain itself.'

I. i. 243. F reads *She is herself a dowry*: but Q is quite intelligible and stronger: 'it is herself that I want, dowry or no dowry; but her perfections are such that they are dowry besides.'

I. i. 270. *wash'd eyes*; usually explained as 'tearful eyes'; but there is no reason why Cordelia should be tearful at leaving her sisters, though every reason why she should be at thus leaving her father. If the reading is right (and the texts agree in it) can it mean 'clear-sighted'?

I. i. 281. Neither the F reading, *the want that you have wanted*, nor the efforts of commentators, make the obscurity of this jingle much less obscure. The general sense is clear; 'you deserve what you are getting.'

I. ii. 21. *top the*; Edward's conj. for Q *tooth'*; F *to'th.*

I. ii. 136. *And out he comes*; so Q. F reads *Pat: he comes*: of which the effectiveness is a good deal diminished by the fact that F omits Q's *Edgar* in the line above. And one may notice as a possibly suspicious and certainly interesting circumstance, that F both here and in a famous line in *Hamlet* (*Now might I do it pat . . .*) inserts a *pat* of which Q knows nothing.

I. ii. 181. *Cf.* again Iago's comments on Othello's character.

I. iii. 21. *With checks as flatteries, when they are seen abus'd*; Tyrwhitt explains, "with checks, as well as flatterers, when they (*i.e.* flatterers) are seen to be abused." The emendators have been busy with the line without much success.

I. iv. 109. *Lady the brach*; so Malone. Q, *Lady o' the brach*, F, *the Lady brach. Cf.* Hotspur in 1 *Henry IV*, III. i. 240. *Lady my brach*: 'brach' was originally a small hound of either sex, but was in Shakespeare's time coming to be used for a bitch.

I. iv. 111. *gall*; so F. Q reads *gull*. The relevance of either is obscure.

I. iv. 225. Q reads *his notion, weaknes, or his discernings are lethergie, sleeping, or waking; ha! sure 'tis not so.* One is tempted to think that Shakespeare had in mind not only mental but physical debility, and wrote *his motion's weakness, or his discernings are lethargie. . . .*

I. iv. 282. *disfeatur'd*; Q reads *disuetur'd*, which is a possible auditory error for the reading given. F reads *disnatur'd*, for which Q's reading would be a possible enough graphical error. With the reading of the text both moral and physical deficiencies are alluded to, with F's reading only the former.

I. iv. 299. *untented*; if this, the reading of Q corrected and F, is right (Q uncorrected reads *untender*), Nares' explanation seems the best: 'not put into a way of cure as a wound is when a surgeon has put a tent into it.' A tent is a roll of lint used in cleansing a fresh wound.

II. ii. 8. *Lipsbury pinfold*; presumably some topical allusion to which we have lost the clue.

II. ii. 30. *sop o' the moonshine*; 'to make a sop of' normally means to set floating (as toast on liquor); it is possible that there may be some allusion to the dish then known as 'eggs in moonshine.' But the real sense required would seem to be one corresponding to 'I'll let daylight into you.'

II. ii. 45. Cf. *Othello*, II. iii.

II. ii. 71. *Which are too intrinse to unloose*; F; Q reads *to intrench to inloose.'* The F reading is not too convincing and commentators have been busy, with small success.

II. ii. 74. *halcyon beaks*; it was a current belief that the halcyon (*i.e.* kingfisher), if hung up, would always swing beak to wind.

II. ii. 78. There seems no reason to emend *smoile* which is read by both Q and F. It is a dialect form of 'smile,' not inappropriate to Kent when he remembers to borrow other accents.

II. ii. 80. Much has been written on Camelot; presumably another topical allusion to a place then famous for its geese.

II. ii. 94-100. An admirable character sketch of Iago.

II. ii. 139. *basest and contemned'st*; Capell's reading: not wholly satisfactory; Q uncorrected reads *belest and contand*, Q corrected, *basest and temnest.*

II. ii. 157-58. *out of heaven's benediction comest To the warm sun*; cf. Heywood's *Dialogues on Proverbs*; *In your rennyng from hym to me, ye runne out of God's blessing into the warm sunne*; *i.e.* from good to worse. Skeat suggested that the proverb refers to the haste of the congregation to leave the shelter of the church, immediately after the priest's benediction, running from God's blessing into the warm sun. This explanation seems as good as any that has been suggested.

II. ii. 161. *miracles*; so F. Q readings are *my rackles* (uncorrected) and *my wracke* (corrected). One would feel happier about the F reading were it not that the Q compositor had no difficulty with *miracle*, either in I. i. 224 or IV. vi. 55.

II. ii. 164-166. *and shall . . . remedies*; many emendations have been proposed to remove the obscurity of the lines, but none can be considered satisfactory. Jennens suggested that Kent is reading disjointed fragments of Cordelia's letter. *From this enormous state* seems to mean 'in this abnormal state of affairs.'

II. iv. 100. *commands her service*; Q uncorrected, *come and tends service*; Q corrected, *commands her service.* F dealing as best it can with Q uncorrected, *commands, tends, service.* The trouble suggests a MS. confusion of *attends her service* and *commands her service.*

II. iv. 170. *tender-hefted*; so F; Q, *tender hested.* Both readings are difficult, and none of the many attempted explanations is very helpful. The inevitable emendation. *tender-hearted* (Pope and Rowe) is quite unconvincing, though it gives no doubt the general required sense.

III. ii. 4. *thought-executing*; usually explained as 'acting with the rapidity of thought,' but this does not seem wholly satisfactory, and something meaning 'more rapid than thought,' such as 'thought-excelling,' would be more pointed.

III. ii. 37. *No I will be the pattern of all patience*; *cf.* the description of Leir by Perillus in the old play:—*But he, the myrrour of mild patience, Puts up all wrongs, and never gives reply.*

III. ii. 58. *concealed centres*; so Q. But there is a good deal to be said for F's *concealing continents*, and, if it were not that it has a little the air of a tinkering for the sake of metre, one would accept it without hesitation.

III. ii. 74-77. *Cf.* Clown's song in *Twelfth Night*, V. i.

III. ii. 95. *I live before his time*; the whole prophecy is perhaps a later addition in the interests of the actor who played the fool. It is an imitation of some lines formerly attributed to Chaucer called '*Chaucer's Prophecy*.' It is suspicious that the conditions of the first two lines are traditionally likely, of the rest very much the reverse; but no doubt one should not expect consistency in doggerel.

III. iv. 53. *knives under his pillow and halters in his pew* (to tempt him to suicide). Theobald pointed out that the allusion is to an incident mentioned in Harsnet's *Declaration.*

III. iv. 75. *pelican daughters, i.e.* daughters who are like the *young* pelicans, feeding on their mother's (in this case father's) life.

III. iv. 101. *sessa*; Malone's emendation; F *Sesey*, Q *caese.* The word occurs in *The Taming of the Shrew*, Induction, l. 6; and elsewhere. But there is no certainty about its meaning.

III. iv. 110. *come on, be true*: so Q uncorrected. The fact that Q corrected reads only *come on* may imply that after this there was a difficult word or words which the corrector gave up in despair, and F deciphered, or conjectured, as (*un*)*button here*, (the usual reading). But the Q reading is defensible enough: 'Off with the lendings, the accidents, and then I shall be truly my self, my bare self.'

III. iv. 138-39. Cp. *The Romance of Sir Bevis of Hamptoun*;—

> "*Rattes and myce and suche small dere,*
> *Was his meate that seuen yere.*"

III. iv. 181. *Childe Rowland to the dark toun came*; F reads *towre*, Q *towne*; as F seems to be the only authority for *tower* (though the other two lines occur among fragments of an old ballad), I have retained Q's reading, though in the northern spelling. But Q also reads *come*, and I suspect that the true reading is *Childe Rowland's to the dark toun come.*

III. vi. 25. Q actually reads *wanst thou eyes, at tral madam.* The reading given is perhaps as little unsatisfactory as any that have been suggested, seeing that we cannot demand coherent sense in this scene. (But? *wanst=wann'st*, i.e., 'grows pale'.)

III. vi. 26. *Come o'er the bourn . . .*; the 'burden' of an old English ballad.

III. vi. 68-69. Both Q and F give the comma after *mongrel* which is usually omitted. Apart from the fact that there is no reason why a mongrel should be grim, the run of the lines seems to need four different types of hound in this line, followed by the two pairs of the next line; and as both Q and F read *him* (F *hym*) I have left it so, the phrase thus meaning 'bitch or dog,' without more violence to grammar than may be expected in this kind of doggerel. But I have to admit that I cannot find either meaning or emendation for *grim.*

III. vi. 75. *Thy horn is dry.* "A horn was usually carried about by every Tom of Bedlam, to receive such drink as the charitable might afford him, with whatever scraps of food they might give him" (Malone), etc.

III. vii. 58-63. F characteristically reads the more ordinary *stick* and *stern* for Q's *rash* and *dearne*, and *bare* for the somewhat mysterious Q *lowd.* But *rash* (to thrust) and *dearne* (dark, dire) are both recognised words, and there seems no reason to change them; and *low'd* (*i.e.* 'lowered,' 'bent') is at least as vivid as *bare.* In line 60 Q uncorrected reads *layd up*, corrected, *bod up.* The F *buoy'd up* may be right, but involves an odd meaning for *buoy'd.*

III. vii. 65. *All cruels else subscrib'd*; so Q; F *subscribe.* Either reading leaves the passage obscure, and many attempts at explanation have been made, none very convincing. *E.g.* 'acknowledge the claims of all creatures, however cruel they may be at other times,' or 'give up all cruel things else' or 'all their other cruelties being yielded or forgiven.'

IV. ii. 12. It is almost irresistibly tempting to adopt Wright's conjecture of *currish terror.* Q uncorrected reads *cowish curre*, corrected, *cowish terrer*, F *cowish terror.* 'Cowish' is an extremely rare word, 'currish' common enough (and occurring, for what it is worth, in Harsnet).

IV. ii. 28. I have kept, very dubiously, the reading of Q corrected. The reading of Q uncorrected *My foote usurps my body*, sounds precisely the pointed but obscure remark which lends itself to such simplifying emendation. Q 2 is clearly moving on the same lines as Q uncorrected, since it reads *My foote usurps my head.* F reads *My foole usurps my body.*

IV. ii. 29. *I have been worth the whistle*; usually interpreted as 'I was once worth something,' an interpretation which is indeed supported by a proverb, 'a poor dog that is not worth the whistling,' but does not seem to have any particular relevance. Goneril has not been complaining of Albany's neglect of her, but of his cowish spirit.

IV. ii. 68. *your manhood mew . . .*; Q uncorrected, *your manhood now*, corrected, *your manhood mew . . .*; I can see neither necessity nor justification for taking 'mew' as an interjection of contempt. Goneril surely means, 'if all that is troubling you is the difference in sex, put off your manhood ('mew'=moult, shed) and I shall be happy to meet you on equal terms.'

IV. iii. 19-32. The passage is not satisfactory, but neither are the guesses at interpretation; so I leave it without adding another stone to the cairn; but inserting one comma.

IV. iv. 6. *century*; Q reads *a centurie is sent forth*, F *a Centery forth.* The word in either form has been taken to mean 'sentry' on the grounds that *century* is an anachronism. But there is no evidence that 'sentry' ever meant anything but a single man on a fixed post of guard, and in any case one man is inadequate for the search. So that the meaning is, I think, clearly, anachronism or no anachronism, simply 'a body of soldiers.'

IV. vi. 92. *well flown, bird in the air*; so Q. F reads *well flown bird; i' the clout, i' the clout*, making Lear revert from the hawk to the arrow.

IV. vi. 96. *Ha, Goneril, ha, Regan*; so Q. F reads *Ha, Goneril with a white beard!* which is certainly much more pointed.

IV. vi. 160. Q reads *dogge, so bade in office*; of interest as showing how corruptions may be due to aural, not visual, error (*cf. the mistresse of Heccat* in I. i. 111 for *mysteries*).

IV. vi. 184. *This a good block*; the Q reading. One cannot be surprised at sudden 'starts' in Lear's speech; but one cannot help feeling that there underlies this phrase a parallel to or amplification of *This great stage of fools*; and Q prints with comma after *fools*, full-stop after *block.*

IV. vi. 215-16. The reading given is that of F. Q reads *Near and on speed for't, the maine descries Standst on the hourly thoughts.* Of this *on speed for't* (*i.e.* for it, the battle) would stand well enough, but the rest is hopeless. F's reading is at least intelligible: 'we expect every hour to see their main body.'

IV. vi. 235. *Lest the infection. . . .*; there is an interesting parallel here to the source of the sub-plot in *Arcadia.*

IV. vi. 273. The actual reading of Q is *and for you her owne for* Venter, Gonorill.' The fact that it makes no sense as it stands seems to be no excuse for omitting it. We may suspect either 'for venture' or 'fore-venter': but the italicisation raises difficulties.

IV. vii. 37. *injurer's*; Q reads *injurious*, F *enemy's.*

V. i. 26. *not bolds the king*; if the reading is right *bolds* must mean 'emboldens,' but the sense is very awkward. Mason's conjecture is tempting, *Not the old king*, since Albany's point appears to be that he will fight against foreign invasion, but cannot feel any enthusiasm in fighting against the wronged king.

V. i. 30. Q, *domestique dore particulars*, which suggests that the true reading at any rate had *particulars* as a noun. Just possibly, *domestic'd o'er particulars.* The reading in the text does not pretend to do more than give the general sense.

V. iii. 24. *the good years.* There is no justification for Hanmer's assumption that this is a corruption of 'goujeres,' a word which existed only in Hanmer's imagination (see N.E.D. *sub voc.*). The word (good-years) "came to be used in imprecatory phrases, as denoting some undefined malefic power or agency." Here there is a very clear reversed allusion to the devouring of the good kine-years by the lean ones in Genesis xli. 18-21.

V. iii. 49. Q uncorrected, *coren bossom*, corrected, *common bossome*. We must I suppose accept the correction, followed by F, with such conviction as we may.

V. iii. 76. *the walls is thine*; a very odd phrase. Theobald read *they all are thine*; I suggest, as graphically easier, *then all is thine*.

V. iii. 144-145. Q *By right of knighthood*. F inserts a line before this, *What safe and nicely I might well delay*, and Q as it stands requires an object for *disdain*. Q may therefore have merely omitted a line, feeble though the line is. (Or ? read *My* for *By*).

V. iii. 169. Q has the remarkable reading *vertues* for F's *vices*.

V. iii. 204. *but another...*; "one more such circumstance only, by amplifying what is already too much, would add to it, and so exceed what seemed to be the limit of sorrow" (Wright).

V. iii. 309-13. F gives the stage-direction for Lear's death after *lookes there*, and assigns *Break heart, I prithee break* to Kent. Q has no direction for the death, but attributes the speeches as in the text, with, I think, far better effect.

Glossary

MANY words and phrases in Shakespeare require glossing, not because they are in themselves unfamiliar, but for the opposite reason, that Shakespeare uses in their Elizabethan and unfamiliar sense a large number of words which seem so familiar that there is no incentive to look for them in the glossary. It is hoped that a glossary arranged as below will make it easy to see at a glance what words and phrases in any particular scene require elucidation. A number of phrases are glossed by what seems to be, in their context, the modern equivalent rather than by lexicographical glosses on the words which compose them.

Act First

SCENE I

line
1 AFFECTED, favoured
6 CURIOSITY, scrutiny of
7 MOIETY, share
11 BRAZED, hardened
12 CONCEIVE, understand
32 OUT, abroad
36 DARKER, hitherto concealed
65 CHAMPAINS, rich plains
77 FELICITATE, happy
81 HEREDITARY, heirs
113 FROM WHOM, by whose influence
115 PROPERTY, relationship
118 GENERATION, children
125 NURSERY, care
137 ADDITIONS, ceremonial due
145 FORK, head
160 BLANK, 'bull's eye'
208 ELECTION MAKES NOT UP, choice cannot be made
217 ARGUMENT, theme
282 PLEATED, folded
304 HIT TOGETHER, act in concert

SCENE II

3 STAND IN THE PLAGUE OF CUSTOM, suffer the disabilities enforced by convention
4 CURIOSITY, fastidiousness
24 SUBSCRIBED, transferred
25 EXHIBITION, maintenance
26 GAD, spur (of the moment)
44 ESSAY, trial
48 FOND, foolish
98-9 WIND ME INTO HIM, gain his confidence ('*me* is 'ethic dative')
120 EXCELLENT FOPPERY, last word in affectation
125 SPHERICAL, of the spheres (*i.e.* the planets)
129 GOATISH, lascivious
131 DRAGON, the constellation Draco
152 SECTARY ASTRONOMICAL, student of astrology
184 PRACTICES, schemes

SCENE IV

2 DEFUSE, confuse
4 RAZ'D, disguised
31 CURIOUS, elaborate
45 CLOTPOLE, dolt
52 ROUNDEST, abruptest
53 A, he
66 FAINT, languid
86 DIFFERENCES, 'your place'
185 MEANS THAT FRONTLET, means that (frowning) brow
196 SHEALED PEASCOD, shelled pea-pod
205 ALLOWANCE, sanction
207 TENDER, securing
WEAL, well-being
213 IT, its
249 BESORT, befit
279 DEROGATE, degenerate
282 THWART, perverse
284 CADENT, falling
FRET, cut
299 UNTENTED, uncleansed
300 FOND, foolish
324 BUZZ, rumour
344 ATTASK'D, blamed

SCENE V

9 KIBES, sores
15 CRAB, crab-apple

Act Second

SCENE I

8 BUSSING, kissing (*i.e.* just touching)
55 GASTED, made aghast
65 PIGHT, determined
78 TUCKET, flourish of trumpets
80 PORTS, gates (or *possibly in the modern sense*)
17 THING OF A QUEASY QUESTION, ticklish design
107 PRACTICE, treachery
112 IN MY STRENGTH, with my authority
124 FROM, away from

SCENE II

14 THREE-SUITED, with (only) three suits
16 ACTION-TAKING, litigious
GLASS, mirror
23 ADDITION, title
31 CULLIONLY, rascally
35 CARBONADO, slash (of meat before broiling)
43 FLESH, draw blood
61 UNBOLTED, unsifted (*i.e.* coarse)
63 JAKES, privy
71 INTRINSE, intricate
74 RENEGE, deny
86 LIKES, pleases
99 DUCKING, bowing
OBSERVANTS, sycophants

Act II Sc. ii —continued

line
100 NICELY, punctiliously
114 CONJUNCT, taking his part
119 FLESHMENT, excitement ('*fleshed* ='having tasted blood')
121 THEIR FOOL, a fool compared to them (in their own opinion)
150 RUBB'D, impeded

SCENE III

10 ELF, tangle
11 PRESENTED, exposed
18 PELTING, petty
19 BANS, curses

SCENE IV

7 CREWEL, worsted (*pun on* 'cruel')
10 NETHER-STOCKS, stockings
30 REEKING POST, sweating messenger
35 MEINY, company
41 DISPLAY'D, behaved
54 TELL, count (*with pun on dolours* (*dollars*) *in line above*)
55 MOTHER, hysteria
87 FETCHES, excuses
104 OFFICE, duty
112 REMOTION, keeping aloof
115 PRESENTLY, at once
118 COCKNEY, squeamish woman
174 SIZES, allowances (*cf.* 'sizar')
33 SPITE OF INTERMISSION, in spite of the fact that he was interrupting
34 PRESENTLY, at once
208 WAGE, contend
215 SUMPTER, pack-horse
223 EMBOSSED, come to a head
244 SLACK, be slack, in attendance on
255 WELL-FAVOUR'D, good-looking
264 ARE ... SUPERFLUOUS, have more than the bare minimum
265 ALLOW NOT, if you do not allow
283 FLAWS, fragments
299 RUFFLE, bluster

Act Third

SCENE I

4 ELEMENT, weather
12 CUB-DRAWN, sucked dry
18 NOTE, knowledge
26 SNUFFS, quarrels
26 PACKINGS, intrigues
29 FURNISHINGS, trappings
39 PLAIN, complain

SCENE II

3 COCKS, weather-cocks
5 VAUNT-COURIERS, fore-runners (*avant-couriers*)
8 GERMINS, seeds
18 SUBSCRIPTION, loyalty
29 LOUSE, be infested with lice
44 GALLOW, terrify
54 SIMULAR, posing

SCENE IV

58 TAKING, malignant charming
67 PENDULOUS, hanging above
98 PLACKET, hole in petticoat
107 UNACCOMMODATED, untrimmed
116 WEB, } diseases of the eye
117 PIN, }
117 SQUINIES, makes to squint
120 'OLD, wold
124 AROINT, avaunt!
130 TODPOLE, tadpole
WATER, sc. newt
132 SALLETS, salads
134 TITHING, district
138 DEER, beasts
181 CHILDE, young noble awaiting knighthood

SCENE V

10 APPROVES, proves
INTELLIGENT, 'in the know'
18 APPREHENSION, seizing

SCENE VI

5 DESERVE, requite
39 BENCH, sit
45 MINIKIN, dainty
69 BRACH, bitch
70 TRUNDLE-TAIL, with curled tail
73 HATCH, half-door
74 WAKES, funeral feasts
75 HORN, beggar's bowl
76 ANATOMIZE, dissect
107 SUFFERANCE, suffering
109 PORTABLE, bearable

SCENE VII

10 FESTINANT, swift
17 QUESTRISTS, seekers
29 CORKY, withered
39 QUICKEN, come to life
40 HOSPITABLE FAVOURS, face of your host
54 COURSE, a 'round' in bear-baiting
58 RASH, thrust
59 LOW'D, bowed
61 STELLED, starry
63 DERNE, dire
98 UNTIMELY, inopportunely
104 ROGUISH, wild

Act Fourth

SCENE I

line
4 ESPERANCE, hope
37 WANTON, thoughtless
53 DAUB, dissemble
63 MOPPING AND MOWING, grimacing
69 SUPERFLUOUS, sated
70 STANDS, withstands

SCENE II

13 UNDERTAKE, act
24 CONCEIVE, take my meaning
42 HEAD-LUGG'D, baited
56 NOISELESS, peaceful
60 PROPER, *i.e.* to the fiend
62 SELF-COVER'D, with real self concealed
68 MEW, put off (*from bird moulting*)

SCENE III

44 CASUALTIES, chances
51 DEAR, important

SCENE IV

3 FUMITER, fumitory
4 HOR-DOCKS, (?) white dock
14 SIMPLES, medicinal herbs
17 REMEDIATE, remedial
26 IMPORTANT, importunate
27 BLOWN, puffed up

SCENE V

25 ŒILLADES, glances (of the eye)

SCENE VI

line
14 GROSS, large
15 SAMPIRE, a herb used in pickles (*mentioned by Drayton as growing well near Dover*)
19 COCK, cock-boat
39 SNUFF, 'fag-end'
42 CONCEIT, imagination
53 AT EACH, end to end
57 BOURN, limit
58 SHRILL-GORGED, shrill-throated
63 BEGUILE, cheat
71 WHELK'D, twisted
81 SAFER, saner
ACCOMMODATE, 'get up'
82 HIS, its
87 PRESS-MONEY, 'King's shilling'
88 CROW-KEEPER, crow-scarer (*or possibly scare-crow*)
91 BROWN BILLS, pikes
117 LUXURY, lust
119 FORKS, legs
120 MINCES VIRTUE, is affectedly virtuous
122 FITCHEW, pole-cat
SOILED, over-fed
130 CIVET, perfume
138 SQUINY, squint
145 CASE, socket
161 BEADLE, constable
169 ABLE, vouch for
192 NATURAL, by birth
195 SECONDS, supporters
212 VULGAR, of common report
242 VOR, warn
243 COSTARD, head
BALLOW, club
278 RAKE UP, scantily bury (*i.e.* rake the ground over)
POST, go-between
281 DEATH-PRACTIS'D, whose death was plotted
283 STIFF, insensitive
284 INGENIOUS, conscious

SCENE VII

7 WEEDS, garments
9 SHORTENS, leaves inadequate time for
17 WIND UP, tune
25 TEMPERANCE, sanity
31 FLAKES, locks of hair
36 PERDU, a sentry placed in a perilous position
61 FOND, crazed
66 MAINLY, entirely
67 SKILL, reason
81 EVEN O'ER, recall
97 POINT, aim
PERIOD, goal

Act Fifth

SCENE I

line
4 CONSTANT, determined
6 DOUBTED, suspected
11 FORFENDED, forbidden
31 QUESTION, to be debated
32 ANCIENT OF WAR, veterans
50 O'ERLOOK, look through
69 STANDS ON ME, it is incumbent on me

SCENE III

49 OF, on to
50 IN OUR EYES, against us
69 COMPEERS, equals
83 ATTAINT, impeachment
122 COPE, encounter
129 MAUGRE, despite
150 PRACTICE, trickery
154 STOPPLE, put the bung in
203 PERIOD, stopping-point
274 FALCHION, sword
280 THIS IS A DULL SIGHT, my eyes are dim